Cambridge Elements

Elements in Early Christian Literature
edited by
Garrick V. Allen
University of Glasgow

THE *PSEUDO-CLEMENTINE* TRADITION

The Hermeneutics of Late-Ancient Sophistic Christianity

Benjamin M. J. De Vos
Ghent University

Shaftesbury Road, Cambridge CB2 8EA, United Kingdom

One Liberty Plaza, 20th Floor, New York, NY 10006, USA

477 Williamstown Road, Port Melbourne, VIC 3207, Australia

314–321, 3rd Floor, Plot 3, Splendor Forum, Jasola District Centre, New Delhi – 110025, India

103 Penang Road, #05-06/07, Visioncrest Commercial, Singapore 238467

Cambridge University Press is part of Cambridge University Press & Assessment, a department of the University of Cambridge.

We share the University's mission to contribute to society through the pursuit of education, learning and research at the highest international levels of excellence.

www.cambridge.org
Information on this title: www.cambridge.org/9781009506687

DOI: 10.1017/9781009506694

© Benjamin M. J. De Vos 2025

This publication is in copyright. Subject to statutory exception and to the provisions of relevant collective licensing agreements, no reproduction of any part may take place without the written permission of Cambridge University Press & Assessment.

When citing this work, please include a reference to the DOI 10.1017/9781009506694

First published 2025

A catalogue record for this publication is available from the British Library

ISBN 978-1-009-50670-0 Hardback
ISBN 978-1-009-50668-7 Paperback
ISSN 2977-0327 (online)
ISSN 2977-0319 (print)

Cambridge University Press & Assessment has no responsibility for the persistence or accuracy of URLs for external or third-party internet websites referred to in this publication and does not guarantee that any content on such websites is, or will remain, accurate or appropriate.

For EU product safety concerns, contact us at Calle de José Abascal, 56, 1°, 28003 Madrid, Spain, or email eugpsr@cambridge.org

The *Pseudo-Clementine* Tradition

The Hermeneutics of Late-Ancient Sophistic Christianity

Elements in Early Christian Literature

DOI: 10.1017/9781009506694
First published online: September 2025

Benjamin M. J. De Vos
Ghent University
Author for correspondence: Benjamin M. J. De Vos, Bmardvos.devos@UGent.be

Abstract: This Element, through detailed example, scrutinizes the exact nature of Christian storytelling in the case of the Greek *Pseudo-Clementines*, or *Klementia*, and examines what exactly is involved in the correct interpretation of this Christian prose fiction as a redefined *pepaideumenos*. In the act of such reconsideration of *paideia*, Greek cultural capital, and the accompanying reflections on prose literature and fiction, it becomes clear that the *Klementinist* exploits certain cases of intertextual and meta-literary reflections on the Greek novelistic fiction, such as Chariton's *Chaereas and Callirhoe* and Achilles Tatius' *Leucippe and Cleitophon*, in order to evoke these reconsiderations of storytelling, interpretive hermeneutics, and one's role as a culturally Greek reader *pepaideumenos*. This Element argues that the *Klementia* bears witness to a rich, dynamic, and Sophistic context in which reflections on *paideia*, dynamics regarding Greek identity, and literary production were neatly intertwined with reflections on reading and interpreting truth and fiction.

Keywords: *Pseudo-Clementines*, *paideia*, Sophistic, Greek narrative prose, Clement of Rome

© Benjamin M. J. De Vos 2025

ISBNs: 9781009506700 (HB), 9781009506687 (PB), 9781009506694 (OC)
ISSNs: 2977-0327 (online), 2977-0319 (print)

Contents

From Clement's Distress …	1
… to Scholarly Distress: Our Sincere Apologies!	4
Objectives of This Element	9
Klementia: Editions, Translations, Concordances	11
Earlier Attitudes towards the *Klementia* as Work of Narrative Prose	14
The Fourth-Century *Klementinist*	20
The *Klementia* as Original Greek Novelistic Prose?	27
The Process of Ἀφελληνισθῆναι *(Aphellênisthênai)*	37
Meta-Literary Tensions Regarding Ἀφελληνισθῆναι *(Aphellênisthênai)*: How (Not) to Read as a Greek	45
The Hermeneutics of the Reader's Identity: Ἀφελληνισθῆναι *(Aphellênisthênai)* as *Re-hellenization*	64
Ἀφελληνισθῆναι *(Aphellênisthênai)* and the Dynamics of Sophistic Christianity	67
Some Concluding Reflections on Future Scholarship	69
Bibliography	75

I Clement, being a Roman citizen, even from my earliest youth was able to live chastely, my mind from my boyhood drawing away the lust that was in me to dejection and distress. For I had a habit of reasoning – how originating I know not – making frequent cogitations concerning death: When I die, shall I neither exist, nor shall any one ever have any remembrance of me, while boundless time bears all things of all men into forgetfulness? And shall I then be without being, or acquaintance with those who are; neither knowing nor being known, neither having been nor being? And has the world ever been made? And was there anything before it was made? ... As I pondered without ceasing these and such like questions – I know not whence arising – I had such bitter grief, that, becoming pale, I wasted away.

Pseudo-Clement of Rome, *Klementia*, 1.1–1.2.1.

From Clement's Distress ...

Distressed, bitter, wasted away. This is how the young pagan protagonist, Clement of Rome, enters the *Pseudo-Clementine* narrative. The *Pseudo-Clementines* is a name given to a cluster of texts which comprises several traditions of this late-ancient narrative. This narrative is presented as an autobiographical account of the young Roman citizen. The two main fourth-century traditions are the *Klementia* (*Klem.*) or *Homilies* (*Hom.*) and the *Recognitions* (*Rec.*). The latter, however, is preserved only as an adapted Latin translation, with the exception of a number of Greek fragments, redacted by Rufinus of Aquileia in the early fifth century.[1] The *Klementia* or *Homilies* is preserved in Greek and divided into twenty books equally termed *Homilies*. Also a Syriac version that seems to incorporate parts of both traditions has been preserved. One manuscript that preserves a version of this Syriac tradition, *British Library Add. 12,150*, is particularly significant, as it provides the oldest textual witness of the *Pseudo-Clementine* narrative, dated to 411 AD.[2] Most scholars agree that these extant versions are rewritings of a hypothetical third-century *Basic Writing* (in German *Grundschrift*, and in French *L'Écrit de Base*): a theory that has inspired many scholars to study and harmonize the several extant *Pseudo-Clementine* traditions to discern the nature of this *Grundschrift*, or of even older sources underlying it.

According to Eusebian tradition, Clement is Peter's third successor as bishop of Rome,[3] though the *Pseudo-Clementine* narrative largely omits this episode of Clement's life. Only a brief reference to his appointment as

---

[1] Rehm and Strecker, *Die Pseudoklementinen I*.
[2] Jones, *The Syriac Pseudo-Clementines*.
[3] Cf. Eusebius, *HE* 5.6.2–4; see also Irenaeus of Lyons, *AH* 3.3.

successor to Peter in Rome appears in Clement's introductory letter to the *Klementia*, addressed to James, bishop of Jerusalem (sections 1–2). The narrative does not mention Clement's death and martyrdom in Chersonesos, present-day Crimea, where he was reportedly tied to an anchor and thrown into the Black Sea. This detail forms part of another fourth-century writing, the *Acta Clementis*.[4]

In the *Pseudo-Clementines*, a homodiegetic ego-narrator, Clement, grapples with doubts about the soul's immortality and the cosmos' infinity. He languishes to such extent that he develops a pallid complexion before finally embarking upon a quest for insight into the true nature of the soul and cosmos. Time and again, he faces disappointment in encounters with magicians and philosophical teachers, who fail to provide the truth he seeks, offering only eristic performance and *dissensus philosophorum*.

One day, Clement overhears an individual preaching about the "True Prophet," a title given to Jesus in the *Pseudo-Clementines*. This Prophet is said to perform miracles in Judea, proclaim the coming Kingdom of God, and reveal the nature of the immortal soul. Intrigued, Clement sets off from Rome to Judea to witness this Prophet with his own eyes. This journey invites the reader to closely accompany him across the Mediterranean. After setting sail for Judea, Clement first arrives in Alexandria,[5] where he debates several philosophers on matters of the divine, truth, and dialectics. There, he encounters Barnabas, a colleague of Peter, who tells him more about the True Prophet and invites him to the port city of Caesarea Stratonis. Here, the distressed young Roman is initiated as a disciple and, eventually, as Peter's successor. Portrayed as the True Prophet's most esteemed student, Peter relieves Clement of his uncertainty and stress regarding the soul and cosmos by introducing him to the teachings of the True Prophet Jesus, who had already died by the time Clement reached Caesarea. Clement writes down – as per request by Peter – the story of his quest for truth, Peter's highly original teachings on humankind, the soul, the cosmos, and God, and details of the apostle's many disputes with Simon Magus. In this narrative, Simon Magus surpasses his portrayal in the Acts of the Apostles (8:9–25) and assumes the status of main opponent and symbolic heretic of early Christianity.[6] These

---

[4] See also Zosimus *Ep.* 2 (P.L. XX, 650). For the reference in Clement's *Passio*, written at the end of the fifth century, see P. G. I, 1053, note 52.

[5] In the *Recognitions*, he meets Barnabas in Rome (*Rec.* I.7–11), after which he travels towards Caesarea.

[6] Cf. Haar, *Simon Magus*; Bremmer, "Simon Magus," 246–270; De Vos, "Paideia, Plato's Sophist," 187–222.

confrontations between Peter and Simon do not concern the subject of magic, but rather focus on extensive expositions and dialectical discussions about God's nature and creation, in addition to the subjects of knowledge, education, and *paideia*. *Paideia* is not simply education, but rather refers to the process of education; the role of rhetoric, philosophy, and literature; the end result of culture; and thus, even the defining aspect of social and cultural identity. As I discuss in depth later on, *paideia* is key to the *Klementia*, and the intellectual exchanges between the main protagonists distinguish this tradition from other early Christian traditions in which these encounters occur, such as the *Apocryphal Acts of Peter*,[7] but also from other *Pseudo-Clementine* traditions due to the more prominent and sophisticated role of *paideia*. The *Pseudo-Clementine* narrative thus presents a distinctive portrayal of a young man's religious–philosophical quest for truth and the ultimate philosophical relief regarding his epistemological and existential distress by means of a reconsideration of *paideia*.

Clement's life story also involves distress over his family, from whom he was separated at a young age. His mother Mattidia, brothers Aquila and Nicetas, and father Faustus were estranged due to a series of unfortunate events. Only in the second part of the narrative does the reader learn that Mattidia's brother-in-law had tried to seduce her, prompting her to fabricate a dream to escape, with her two older sons, to Athens to avoid shaming her husband's family. A subsequent shipwreck left Mattidia on the island of Aradus, with her children sold as slaves and later adopted by the Jewish woman Justa (cf. *Klem.* 13.7).[8] Receiving no news of his family, the father searched for them but found himself lost in the eastern Mediterranean. Clement, the youngest son, was left alone in Rome. With Peter's help, whom Clement considers a foster-parent, the eponymous hero is later reunited with his family. The *Pseudo-Clementine* narrative presents an original framework of several recognition scenes, leading it to be called the first – and only surviving – Christian novel from the earliest centuries, or at least a Christian response to Greek novelistic prose fiction.

Before further defining this literature, its context, and this Element's objectives, it should be noted that its unique literary character, narrative structure, and original religious–philosophical content have sparked

---

[7] For an overall comparison of these encounters between Peter and Simon, see Côté, *Le thème de l'opposition*, 135–253; for an insightful discussion regarding the *Actus Vercellenses* in combination with the *Pseudo-Clementine* narrative, see Filippini, "Atti apocrifi petrini," 17–41.

[8] For a discussion of Justa in relation to the Syrophoenician woman from *Mark* 7:25–30 and *Matt.* 15:21–28, see Forger, "Interpreting the Syrophoenician Woman," 132–166.

considerable debate. This pertains, among other aspects, to the precise definition of the "Christian" nature of the *Pseudo-Clementines*. As I discuss in this Element, we are dealing with original reflections of a late-ancient, Judaizing author contemplating the role of Jesus as a prophet and the dialogue between different expressions of Judaism and Christianity. For the sake of clarity, I refer to the *Pseudo-Clementines* as "Christian" fiction, although I emphasize that the *Klementia* should be understood as a particularly original and far from marginal fourth-century expression, in which the author clearly presents Moses and Jesus as incarnations of the True Prophet proclaiming the same truth, self-identifies not as Christian but as *Iudaios* and *theosebès*, and engages deeply with the hermeneutics of both Scripture and Gospel traditions. The precise nature of "Christian" and "Jewish-Christian" has led to extensive discussions among scholars and has had implications across various fields of research. Some scholars have even felt the need to apologize when addressing the *Pseudo-Clementines* from a historicizing perspective, due to the many methodological issues regarding this literature.

... to Scholarly Distress: Our Sincere Apologies!

We particularly observe this tendency in studies on the history of Christianity and Judaism, where distinct views on the narrative have largely been approached in terms of its potential historical value regarding hypothetical older layers of (Jewish-)Christian theories underlying the extant versions. In the first of his two lectures delivered at Trinity College Dublin in 1901, the theologian and, at that time, professor of Dogmatic Theology at King's College London, Arthur C. Headlam, remarked:

> Some apology is I think due for asking your attention to a subject which is only a bypath of Church history. My excuse must be that when I received the kind invitation of your Divinity Professors, the Clementine literature happened to be the work on which I was engaged; and although in my opinion this literature is out of the current of the main Church life, and although, as Prof. Harnack insists, it has had little influence on the development of Christian doctrine or life, yet it has been raised into adventitious importance by much modern speculation, and it is necessary for every investigator of early Christianity to decide for himself what historical value these documents may possess.[9]

Thirteen years earlier, Adolf Harnack – to whom Headlam refers – downplayed the pivotal value of the *Pseudo-Clementine* corpus (specifically

---

[9] Headlam, "The Clementine Literature," 41.

the *Klementia*), as assigned earlier by Ferdinand Christian Baur. Baur and the Tübingen School regarded the *Klementia* as an important early Christian witness (dated to the second century on his account) of his dialectical theory that second-century Christianity represented a synthesis of two factions. On one side, he approached Peter's character as a *persona* of the original "Petrine," law-observing Jewish-Christian party and, on the other, he linked Simon Magus' character to the "Pauline," law-rejecting, gentile-Christian faction.[10] According to Harnack,[11] however, the *Pseudo-Clementines* contributed absolutely nothing to the field of the history of early Christianity or the development of the Catholic Church. This rather negative view of the corpus' historical value seemingly caused some embarrassment for Headlam. Later scholars, too, expressed hesitation about the historical value of the *Pseudo-Clementine* literature, often feeling the need to justify their interest in it. About sixty years later, Walter Ullmann, then a Fellow of Trinity College Cambridge, wrote about the historical–theological significance of the *Epistola Clementis*, one of the three introductory writings of the *Klementia*. Ullmann, too, felt compelled to apologize for his choice of subject. The explicit reason given for this apology relates to the copious volume of secondary literature that had already appeared regarding the *Pseudo-Clementines*:

> The choice of this subject may well cause some surprise: What – another discussion of the Pseudo-Clementines? Can, with our present-day knowledge, anything be usefully added that has not already been said in the copious literature on the cluster of problems surrounding this novelistic product?[12]

Before I myself feel obliged to apologize for offering yet another discussion on this literature, it should be noted that Ullmann expressed the discomfort that he had (or at least pretended to have) in considering this literature as theological work and "novelistic product," as well as in considering its value within the fields of church history, theology, and the history of religion. The unique theories expressed by Peter's character, particularly in the Greek *Klementia*, such as the theory that false pericopes corrupted the original oral Mosaic Law with God's approval (e.g., *Klem.* 2.38; 2.51), that God created the Evil One by mixing the four basic elements (*Klem.* 19.12; 20.8), the emphatic silence on the crucifixion and resurrection, and

---

[10] Baur, "Die Christuspartei," 61–206.
[11] Harnack, *Dogmengeschichte*, 264–270.
[12] Ullmann, "The Significance of the Epistola Clementis," 295; cf. Ullmann, "Some Remarks," 330.

the portrayal of Jesus as one of the manifestations of the True Prophet (along with Adam and Moses; *Klem.* 1.47), in addition to the absence of the term Χριστιανός [*Christianós*] in the *Klementia*,[13] quickly led the corpus to be labelled unorthodox and reduced to the status of marginal work. The theologian and Church of England clergyman, Charles Bigg, even wrote in poetic, almost ominous, terms about the "sect" from which the *Klementia* were thought to have originated:

> When the Light of the World had arisen they turned aside after the marsh-fires of an idle antiquated mysticism and a gross and barbarous superstition and so fell deeper and deeper into the mire.[14]

Bigg sharply criticized the seriousness of some theological–philosophical doctrines in the *Klementia*, particularly the idea of God having an anthropomorphic, corporeal form and six infinite extensions (*Klem.* 17.9.3–4), which he considered "the farthest point in the realm of nonsense ever reached by any human being."[15] While I approach this work from a literary–critical and philosophical perspective, earlier theological research, considering the *Clementines* as a rather marginal expression, has nevertheless significantly influenced later perspectives on this work in scholarship on the Greek novel, ancient rhetoric, and ancient philosophy. I argue that the *Pseudo-Clementine* narrative has not yet been sufficiently appreciated as an original expression of Christian fiction. Headlam, for instance, called the hypothetical *Grundschrift*'s author "a curious, versatile, unequally developed mind" from the late second or early third century. He noted that:

> [a]s a story the work was a success, as a contribution to serious thought it was a failure. Harnack is right in setting it aside in working out the development of Christian thought. ... The Clementine literature is outside the current of Church life.[16]

The biblical scholar and (at that time) Episcopalian priest, Richard Pervo, unlike Headlam, characterized the long-winded storyline and drawn-out disputes of the *Pseudo-Clementines* as "a smear-piece no less dreadful than it is tedious."[17] This view stemmed from the *Quellenkritik* approach, which has dominated *Pseudo-Clementine* research for many decades, even centuries. Scholars have focused on identifying hypothetical older, literary, philosophical, and (Jewish-)Christian sources from the first and second

---

[13] Except for *Rec.* IV.20.4, a passage which could have been inserted by Rufinus himself.
[14] Bigg, "The Clementine Homilies," 192.
[15] Bigg, "The Clementine Homilies," 163.
[16] Headlam, "The Clementine Literature," 58.
[17] Pervo, "The Ancient Novel," 707.

centuries, or in other words, traces of early (Jewish-)Christian doctrines beyond the narrative façade, rather than approaching the extant third- and fourth-century *Pseudo-Clementine* versions in their own right. This extensive excavation, diverse opinions about the often-hypothetical sources, and lack of any final conclusion have often led researchers to positions of confusion when conducting *Pseudo-Clementine* scholarship. In 1888, Adolf Harnack summarized these problematic issues in a single sentence that "auf diesem Gebiete nicht weniger als Alles noch im Dunkeln liegt" ("in this field, nothing less than everything remains in darkness"),[18] among which regarding the composition of the corpus. More than 100 years ago, the biblical scholar Rendel Harris also stated that "[a]mongst the problems there is none that rivals in perplexity and obscurity the question of the origin of the so-called Pseudo-Clementine literature."[19] In 1958, the historian of religion, Hans Joachim Schoeps, even considered the biblical *Quellenkritik* as child's play (*ein Kinderspiel*) compared to research into the *Pseudo-Clementines*.[20]

This problematic terrain, reinforced by academic compartmentalization, has deeply influenced studies in ancient narrative, especially the ancient novel, and early and late-ancient Christian literature. A review of general reference works on ancient narrative, Greek prose fiction, and Jewish and Christian narrative reveals that the *Pseudo-Clementines* have often been neglected or insufficiently discussed, primarily treated from a historical perspective. Mark J. Edwards' 1992 comment that the *Pseudo-Clementines* "are treated all too frequently as material for historians, not for critics," unfortunately remains relevant today.[21]

This focus on historical value relates to the term "pseudo," as the narrative, created only in the third and fourth centuries, is not considered an authentic autobiographical writing by Clement of Rome.[22] Recently, scholars have argued, with good reason, to advance the simpler denomination *Clementina*. This debate reflects an underlying lack of consensus on the genre, approach, and disciplinary focus of the text. Nonetheless, as this Element discusses, significant value remains in studying it as an original Christian and philosophical narrative that engages with and positions itself in narrative tradition to which expressions of Greek erotic prose also belong.

---

[18] Harnack, *Dogmengeschichte*, 265–266.
[19] Harris, "Notes," 125.
[20] Schoeps, "Die Pseudoklementinen," 4.
[21] Edwards, "The *Clementina*," 459.
[22] See already Epiphanius' view in his *Panarion*, 26.16 and 30.15.1.

This Element does not address whether the *Pseudo-Clementine* literature renders a mere *fictive* narrative or whether all possible hypothetical sources can be distilled. Instead, we shall raise alternative questions concerning its literary character and rhetorical dynamics, particularly its strategies of veracity and credibility. The Greek *Klementia* in particular provides sufficient markers of fictionality, guiding educated ancient readers towards make-believe.[23] This concept refers to a set of hermeneutical techniques within the texts and to how they impact the reader response dynamic, establishing complex relations to truth, as can also be observed in so-called Greek novelistic prose fiction, such as Chariton's *Chaereas and Callirhoe* and Achilles Tatius' *Leucippe and Cleitophon*. These novels simultaneously encourage belief in the world as created and signal in sophisticated manner the artificiality of this same world. The same, I argue, occurs in the *Klementia*, shaping expectations about the ways in which the work was intended to be read, or, in other words, the *hermeneutics of reading*. I would like to clarify that the dynamics of the relationship between encouraging belief in the world as created and confronting its artificiality might differ in the case of a novel attributed to a historical Christian figure and martyr compared to that of the Greek novel and its fictional characters. However, the complexity of the reading hermeneutics, their strategies, and the presence of features in the *Pseudo-Clementines* that are also strongly present in the Greek novels provide a compelling basis for comparison regarding the notion of fiction. By paying attention to these strategies, we can better analyze the different techniques deployed by the *Klementinist* to present Christian prose, how the reader is anticipated to react to these strategies regarding truth and belief of and within the work, the notion of storytelling, and the hermeneutics of fiction in general, which have so far been neglected by strictly historical approaches.

In recent decades, there have been several calls for new approaches: not only in the field of the history of Christianity and Judaism, but also in literary studies about the ancient novel and early Christian and Jewish narratives. Recently, Stanley F. Jones noted: "When the *Klementia* is compared with other New Testament apocryphal literature, the author's quite exceptional literary abilities cannot be overlooked."[24] It is high time the *Pseudo-Clementine* literature receives its deserved attention from literary and philosophical critics alike. This Element addresses the need for

---

[23] Morgan, "Make Believe," 175–229.
[24] Jones, "Introduction to the *Pseudo-Clementines*," 36.

Pseudo-Clementine studies within these fields of ancient narrative, ancient novel, and Jewish and Christian narratives, by focusing on the original literary qualities and fictional strategies of the Greek *Klementia*.

Objectives of This Element

First and foremost, storytelling and the hermeneutics of interpreting stories shall represent a key focus of our attention. The Greek tradition, more than other *Pseudo-Clementine* versions, engages with storytelling on multiple levels. Its protagonists share stories about their lives, deceive through fabricated stories, and recognize each other through these stories. Clear reflections are offered on the truth of narratives and stories and, moreover, on the hermeneutics of interpreting them. This occurs not only on the level of the characters' own memories and life stories and their interpretation by other characters but also on a meta-discursive level, where the reader is provided with a hermeneutical framework for interpreting storytelling and narrative traditions. Peter thus discusses distinct renderings and interpretations of the Scriptures and the notion that false pericopes exist within the written Mosaic Law. One must be aware of these false pericopes in order to correctly interpret the Scriptures. Implicitly, the *Klementia* also offers reinterpretations of Gospel traditions through Peter's discussions and teachings. On a meta-narrative level, passages about Clement's autobiography enter into a hypertextual relationship with Platonic myths,[25] including the Phaedran myth of the charioteer (245c–249d) and the Myth of Er from the *Republic* (614–621). These hypotexts provide insight into how these passages require interpretation by the reader. Similar meta-narrative engagement can also be observed in relation to certain expressions of Greek novelistic prose, notably Chariton's *Chaereas and Callirhoe* and Achilles Tatius' *Leucippe and Cleitophon*. Several recognition scenes in the *Klementia* display hypertextual and meta-literary relationships with these novels and, more generally, with the tradition of Greek erotic prose, and offer additional reflections on the *Klementinist's* insights into Christian storytelling and the related fictional aspect. These relationships are expected to be identified and interpreted by well-trained readers versed in relevant intricacies of storytelling and proper hermeneutics.

---

[25] In this case, I follow Genette's definition of *intertextuality* as the relationship between textual witnesses by means of allusions and quotations, as well his discussion of the dynamics of *hypertextuality*, *hypotexts*, and *hypertexts*. Hypertextuality refers to any relationship that connects a text B (the hypertext) to a prior text A (the hypotext), in a manner that is not that of commentary (Genette, *Palimpsests*, sp. 1–6; Allen, *Intertextuality*, 104–111).

Second, I shall elaborate on the readership, particularly the *implied reader*, as well as their relationship to strategies of fiction and belief in and of the work. Drawing on Wolfgang Iser's aesthetic reader-response criticism,[26] I examine how the *Klementinist* text prompts the reader to consider moral, cultural, and meta-literary issues. The *implied reader* differs from any *actual reader*, "who may be unable or unwilling to occupy the position of the implied reader."[27] A key expectation of the *implied reader* regards the cultural capital of *paideia* itself, requiring the reader to hold *pepaideumenos* status. I argue that the *Klementia*, more than other *Pseudo-Clementine* versions, addresses what it means to be (Jewish-)Christian in relation to Greek *paideia*, particularly in terms of Greek culture, education, and *Bildung*. The reader is confronted with several assumptions regarding literature, fiction, and truth when reading Greek prose fiction, a point which is questioned within the *Klementia*. These assumptions, moreover, are linked to reflections on culture and education, therefore representing *paideia*. The *Klementinist* does not simply reject Greek *paideia* but redefines it from within as *pepaideumenos*, expressed on a literary, rhetorical, and philosophical level, alongside religious considerations. The presence of Plato's dialogues and references to Greek novelistic prose are intended for recognition by the reader, in addition to reinterpretations of Scripture and Gospel tradition. This Element shall, through detailed example, scrutinize Christian storytelling and explore what exactly is involved in the correct interpretation of Christian prose fiction as a redefined *pepaideumenos*. In reconsidering *paideia*, Greek cultural capital, and the accompanying reflections on prose literature and fiction, it becomes clear that the *Klementinist* exploits hypertextuality and meta-literary reflections on Greek novelistic fiction in order to evoke these reconsiderations of storytelling, interpretive hermeneutics, and one's role as a culturally Greek reader-*pepaideumenos*. A key concept here involves the distinctive condition of "de-Greekness" (ἀφελληνισθῆναι; *Klem.* 13.9), exploring what it means (not) to write, read, and interpret Christian prose as *pepaideumenos*.

Case studies of the *Klementia* invite us to delve deeper into the notion of Christian fiction and storytelling. The *Klementinist* narrative framework has often been considered as "adopted" from non-Christian novels.

---

[26] Iser, *Der Akt des Lesens*.
[27] Baldick, "Implied Reader," 123. There are several references to the *Pseudo-Clementines* by contemporary and later, *actual readers* (such as Eusebius, Epiphanius, Photius), primarily concerning the question of whether this testimony was indeed authored by Clement of Rome himself. However, these discussions often remain brief and it is, at times, difficult to pinpoint to which particular tradition of the *Pseudo-Clementine* they are referring.

I contend, however, that it is original, with the *Klementinist* offering deliberate meta-reflections on novelistic storytelling distinct from other expressions of (non-Christian) novelistic fiction, particularly Greek erotic novels. I argue that the *Klementia* bears witness to a rich, dynamic, and Sophistic context in which reflections on *paideia*, Greek identity dynamics, and literary production neatly intertwine with reflections on truth and the production of fiction.

Last but not least, this Element seeks not only to offer a fresh perspective on the *Klementia* as Christian – even novelistic – prose fiction, but also to assist readers in navigating the complex circuits of past scholarship. To better understand the *Klementia*'s role as late-ancient fiction, I shall first offer a more extensive *state-of-the-art* cataloguing of earlier insights into its possible context and how it was later approached as an expression of fiction, in relation to other *Pseudo-Clementine* traditions and other Christian and non-Christian literature from the earliest centuries. I shall also provide an overview of the various extant manuscripts, editions, and translations, to assist readers to navigate the corpus of *Pseudo-Clementine* scholarship.

Klementia: Editions, Translations, Concordances

The title *Homilies* or *Klementia* refers to three introductory writings (*Peter's letter to James* [*EpPt*], the *Diamartyria* or *Adjuration* [*D* or *Adj*], *Clement's letter to James* [*EpCl*]), along with the narrative proper divided into twenty books, also called *Homilies* [abbreviated *Hom.* or *Klem.*]. Recent scholarship favors *Klementia*, rather than *Homilies*, as it appears in a tenth-century manuscript of the narrative (Codex Parisinus *gr. 930*) and in two eleventh-century sermons by Nicon Monachos.[28] However, *Homilies* remains firmly established in scholarship, despite methodological pitfalls. Besides possible confusion regarding the genre of *homilistic literature*, the title *Homilies* instigated the deeply rooted idea that it would have better preserved Peter's sermons (*homilies*) from the *Grundschrift* while the *Recognitions* better preserved the framework of the recognition scenes.

The first prefatory writing is Peter's letter to James [*EpPt*], urging that his collection of teachings be revealed only to initiated individuals. A note authored by James constitutes the second writing [*D* or *Adj*], and

---

[28] Cf. Jones, "Photius's Witness," 353–354; Rufinus, in the preface of his Latin *Recognitions*, apologizes for not including a translation of the *Letter of Clement to James*. He claims to have translated it before. Photius (in the ninth century) was most likely aware of versions of the *Recognitions* that began with the *EpCl*.

relates James reading Peter's letter aloud to the seventy elders, with these teachings to be carefully shared only with those who are both pious and circumcised. An oath – by earth, water, and air – is taken, mandating the initiates to take utmost care of the writings. The third writing [*EpCl*] is Clement's letter to the "Bishop of bishops, who rules Jerusalem" (*EpCl* 1.1), James, recounting Peter's final injunctions before his death and Clement's appointment as Peter's successor in the See of Rome.

Two key medieval manuscripts of the Greek *Klementia* are the aforementioned Codex Parisinus *gr.930* (P) and the Vaticanus Ottobonianus *gr.443* (O), held in the *Bibliothèque nationale de France* (BnF) and the *Biblioteca Apostolica Vaticana*, respectively. The P-manuscript, dated to the tenth to twelfth century (with greater consensus on the tenth century), breaks off at *Klem.* 19.14.3. In the sixteenth century, this manuscript already belonged to *la Bibliothèque royale de Fontainebleau* (n°328, 1648, 2874). The O-manuscript was most likely redacted between 1562 and 1564 (probably in Trient or Venice) by Nikolaos Turrianos and his unnamed assistant, who were responsible for the relevant copy of the *Klementia*, and by Andreas Darmarios, who copied the other texts within the manuscript, among which is a selection of Gregory of Nyssa's writings. It likely belonged to the Spanish Jesuit Francisco Torres, who referenced it to inform his *Adversus Centuriatores* (1572) against the *Centuriators of Magdeburg* (written by Luther's pupil M. Flacius), and for his commentaries on the *Apostolic Constitutions*. In 1837, Albert R. M. Dressel "rediscovered" this manuscript, consulting it for his 1853 edition of the *Klementia*.[29]

In 1672, Jean Baptiste Cotelier(us) published the first printed edition of the *Klementia*, based on the incomplete P-manuscript, in his *SS. Patrum qui temporibus apostolicis floruerunt*.[30] Further editions followed by Albert Schwegler (1847),[31] Albert R. M. Dressel (1853),[32] and Paul Anton de Lagarde (1865).[33] The most recent critical version, by Bernhard Rehm and revised by Georg Strecker, remains a solid basis for studies.[34] Several, sometimes outdated, translations of the *Klementia* exist, including the 1886 English translation by Smith, Peterson, and Donaldson within the ANF-series (though caution is warranted when consulting it),[35] alongside

---

[29] Dressel, *Clementis Romani*.
[30] Cotelier, *SS. Patrum* (Vol. 1), 529–746.
[31] Schwegler, *Clementis Romani*.
[32] Dressel, *Clementis Romani*.
[33] Lagarde, *Clementina*.
[34] Rehm and Strecker, *Die Pseudoklementinen I*.
[35] Roberts and Donaldson, *Ante-Nicene Christian Library Vol. XVII*, 1–340.

fragments translated by Robert McL. Wilson from the original German fragmentary translation of Johannes Irmscher and Georg Strecker.[36] A partial English translation by Curtis Hutt and Jenni Irving also exists.[37] In the latter two cases, the editors have made selections of the *Klementia*, reflecting their *quellenkritische* points of view. For example, Hutt and Irving group passages concerning women in the *Pseudo-Clementines*, which would have represented a hypothetical source underlying the *Grundschrift*, and attach an imaginative name to it: *The Sorrows of Mattidia*.[38]

In 1902, Hajo Uden Meyboom provided the only complete Dutch translation (in a synoptic version with a translation of the *Recognitions*).[39] In addition to the excellent French translation of both the *Klementia* and *Recognitions* in the 2005 *Écrits Apocryphes Chrétiens* series (under the meticulous auspices of the *Association pour l'Étude de la Littérature Apocryphe* [AELAC] and the editors Pierre Geoltrain and Jean-Daniel Kaestli),[40] there is the earlier 1933 French translation of the *Klementia* by the pseudonymous André Siouville[41] and a fragmentary translation by Abbé Étienne Maistre dating to 1883–1884.[42] In 2010 and revised in 2015, Jürgen Wehnert edited a complete German translation of the *Klementia*.[43] Select fragments of the *Klementia* have been translated into Swedish by Reidar Hvalvik and Karl Olav Sandnes in 2011,[44] and into Italian in the 2018 work of Marco Zambon.[45] In 2023, Antonio Piñero and Gonzalo del Cerro edited a critical edition of the *Klementia* and provided a Spanish translation in the *Hechos Apócrifos de los Apóstoles* series.[46]

In addition to the Greek version, a Syriac version of (part of) the *Klementia* is preserved mainly within a 411-manuscript from Edessa (*British Library add. 12,150*).[47] This manuscript includes *Klem.* 10.1–12.24

---

[36] Irmscher and Strecker, "The Pseudo-Clementines," 483–541; Irmscher and Strecker, "Die Pseudoklementinen," 439–488.
[37] Hutt, *The Sorrows*.
[38] Hutt, *The Sorrows*, 7.
[39] Meyboom, *De Clemens-Roman*.
[40] Le Boulluec, "Homélies de Pseudo-Clément," 1215–1589.
[41] Siouville, *Les Homélies*.
[42] Maistre, *Saint Clément*.
[43] Wehnert, *Pseudoklementinische Homilien*; Wehnert, *Der Klemensroman*.
[44] Hvalvik and Sandnes, "Pseudo-Klemens homilier."
[45] Zambon, "Apprendere qualcosa di sicuro (ps. Clem. *Klem.* I 2, 1)," 13–48.
[46] Piñero and del Cerro, *Hechos apócrifos*.
[47] Jones ("Introduction to the *Pseudo-Clementines*," 11) notes that this manuscript already contains "quite a few scribal errors," which could indicate that the Greek was already translated a bit earlier. However, I argue that it is also possible that the Syriac version was written simultaneously alongside the Greek version.

and 13.1–14.12, in addition to *Rec.* I.1–IV.1.14,[48] forming yet another distinct textual unity. While my focus is on the Greek *Klementia*, comparisons, where possible, with the Syriac version help better understand the redactional choices of the Greek *Klementinist*. Based on the *British Library Add. 12,150* and a Greek parallel-text, Wilhelm Frankenberg produced a textual edition,[49] seventy-six years subsequent to Paul de Lagarde's 1861 edition of the Syriac version,[50] for which he also consulted *Add. 14,609*. In 2014, Joseph Glen Gebhardt and Stanley Jones each edited an English translation of the Syriac *Clementines*.[51]

To assist in the study of the Greek *Klementia*, William Chawner published an index of *Noteworthy Words and Phrases* in 1893,[52] and Georg Strecker, almost 100 years later, edited a comprehensive concordance of the Greek, Latin, and Syriac versions of the *Klementia* and *Recognitions*.[53]

Earlier Attitudes towards the *Klementia* as Work of Narrative Prose

It is not within my scope to offer a detailed *status quaestionis* of earlier scholarship, especially regarding the aforementioned *Quellenkritik*, (potential) textual history, and historical context of the several *Quellen*. This has been extensively covered by Stanley F. Jones,[54] Jürgen Wehnert,[55] Frédéric Manns,[56] Frédéric Amsler,[57] Jan N. Bremmer,[58] and Benjamin M. J. De Vos and Danny Praet,[59] not to mention the several recent introductions to monographs on the *Pseudo-Clementines* by Meinolf Vielberg,[60] Dominique Côté,[61] Nicole Kelley,[62] and Patricia Duncan.[63] I aim to highlight key

---

[48] The Syriac passages of *Klem.* 12.6.4, 12.6.8–7.1, and 12.7.6–8.3 are also preserved in the thirteenth-century *Cambridge University Library add. 2,023* (folios 60b–61a).
[49] Frankenberg, *Die syrischen Clementinen*.
[50] Lagarde, *Clementis Romani*.
[51] Gebhardt, *The Syriac Clementine*; Jones, *The Syriac Pseudo-Clementines*.
[52] Chawner, *Index of Noteworthy Words and Phrases*.
[53] Strecker, *Die Pseudoklementinen III*; for a few corrections of this concordance, see Jones, "PsCl Concordances," 126–128.
[54] Jones, "A History of Research," 1–33; 63–96.
[55] Wehnert, "Literarkritik," 268–301.
[56] Manns, "Les Pseudo-Clémentines," 157–184.
[57] Amsler, "État de la recherche," 25–45.
[58] Bremmer, "*Pseudo-Clementines*," 236–249.
[59] De Vos and Praet, "The *Pseudo-Clementines*," 1–36.
[60] Vielberg, *Klemens*, 11–23.
[61] Côté, *Le thème de l'opposition*, 7–19.
[62] Kelley, *Knowledge and Authority*, 1–27.
[63] Duncan, *Novel Hermeneutics*, 1–19.

points regarding the *Klementia* as an original narrative work, considering past scholarship and my approach to this expression of Christian fiction.

The *Klementia* has often been studied in relation to the *Recognitions*. A much-debated question in the nineteenth and twentieth centuries concerned which of the two deserves priority status, and which tradition had influenced the other? These questions were raised by the so-called *Benutzungshypothese*. For example, in 1844, Adolph Schliemann stated that the *Recognitions* were a later revision of the *Klementia*.[64] Four years later, in response, Adolf Hilgenfeld suggested the opposite.[65]

Another theory gained ground in the late nineteenth century, mainly through Richard Lipsius: the *Grundschrifthypothese*.[66] This theory suggests that both *Clementine* traditions shared a common, but lost, *Basic Writing*. Lipsius, moreover, argued that the *Recognitions* were based on a mid-second-century source called *Periodoi Petrou dia Klementos grafeisa* or *Anagnorismoi Klementos* (including the *EpCl*). The older, underlying (anti-Pauline and anti-Gnostic) source or *Basic Writing* would have been the hypothetical *Kerygmata Petrou* (including *EpPt, D*, ten books about Peter's disputes with Simon in Caesarea, the latter's flight to Rome, and the role of Clement).[67]

Most scholars promptly agree upon the existence of a *Grundschrift*, but disagree on its appearance, place of origin,[68] authorship,[69] and its precise relationship to the *Benutzungshypothese* (a potential direct dependence between the *Klementia* and *Recognitions* distinct from a direct relationship with the *Grundschrift*). The *Grundschrift* was probably known as the *Periodoi Petrou* or *Travels of Peter*, with *Periodoi* also referring to *Orbits*, referring to the work's anti-astrological stance. This view is based on a reference, possibly by Origen (as it occurs in

---

[64] Schliemann, *Die Clementinen*, 252–253; 316–325.
[65] Hilgenfeld, *Die Clementinischen*, 45, 57.
[66] Lipsius, *Die Quellen*.
[67] Not to be confused with the *Kerygma Petrou* as quoted by Clement of Alexandria (e.g., *Strom*. 1.29.182.3; 2.15.68.2). For the *Kerygmata Petrou*, see Schneemelcher, "Das Kerygma," 34–41, for a translation in German; Norelli, "Situation," 63–71, for a discussion; and Cambe, *Kerygma Petri*, for a critical edition and a translation in English.
[68] For example, according to Waitz (*Pseudoklementinen*, 74–75), the *Grundschrift* was written in Rome; according to Hort (*Judaistic Christianity*), Schmidt (*Studien*, 313), and Cullmann ("Le problème," 156–157), in Transjordania; according to Cirillo ("Jacques de Jérusalem," 179) and Jones ("The Genesis," 204), in Coele-Syria, in particular Apamea.
[69] For example, according to Hort (*Judaistic Christianity*, 87–88), the *Basic Writer* was an Elchesaite Jewish-Christian; according to Schmidt (*Studien*, 288), a former Jewish-Christian converted to Catholicism; according to Headlam ("The Clementine Literature," 55), a Catholic without any contact with Jews; according to Schoeps ("Astrologisches," 98), "einem katholischen Christen."

the anthology *Philocalia* 23.21–22, edited by Basil of Caesarea and Gregory of Nazianzus), to the fourteenth book of the *Periodoi Petrou*, which discusses a conversation between Clement and his father Faustus in Laodicea. Luigi Cirillo suggests this aligns with *Rec.* X.10–13 and considers it a reference to the *Grundschrift*.[70]

The source-critical focus has closely accompanied the *Grundschrifthypothese*. Scholars often divide the *Klementia*, *Recognitions*, and the hypothetical *Grundschrift* into older, mostly hypothetical sources believed to reflect early "Jewish-Christianity." Proposed sources for the *Grundschrift* or the *Klementia* and *Recognitions* include the much debated *Kerygmata Petrou* (*KP*), the source of *Rec.* I.27–71, a lost Jewish *Disputationsbuch*, the lost *Syntagma* of Hippolytus, a lost Greek or Jewish-Hellenistic novel – to which I will later return – and extant sources such as (pseudo-)Bardaisan's *Book of the Laws of the Countries* (*BLC*) or the *Acts of Peter*. These reconstructions of the *Pseudo-Clementine* textual history have sparked disagreement among scholars, as is evident in many dated and even more recent contributions. For example, Hilgenfeld argued that the *KP* (just as the *EpPt* and *Adj*) was a source later combined with the *Periodoi* (which was, according to Hilgenfeld, a source distinct from the *Grundschrift*), resulting in the hypothetical *Anagnorismoi* and then finally in the *Recognitions*, which were later reworked into the *Klementia*.[71] Oscar Cullmann also propounded the *KP* as "le noyau même," and as one of the oldest sources of early Christianity (or, as he calls it, Gnostic Jewish-Christianity), later reworked into the *Periodoi Petrou* as distinct from the *Grundschrift*.[72] Scholars like Arthur Headlam, John Chapman, and Eduard Schwartz rejected *KP*'s existence.[73] Recent scholars, including Josep Rius-Camps, Jürgen Wehnert, Luigi Cirillo, and Bernard Pouderon, show ongoing *dissensus theologicorum philologorumque* on the genesis and textual history of the *Pseudo-Clementine* literature.[74]

To what extent are reconstructions of such a *stemma* useful? Does the theory of a *Grundschrift* used independently by both the *Klementia* and

---

[70] Cirillo, "Les sources," 241; cf. Pouderon, "Origène," 87–103.
[71] Hilgenfeld, *Die Clementinischen*, 44–45; 52–81. Other scholars, such as Schmidt (*Studien*, 286–288), state that the *Recognitionist*, unhappy with the *Klementia*, reworked the *Grundschrift*.
[72] Cullmann, "Le problème," 472.
[73] Headlam, "The Clementine Literature," 50; Chapman, "On the Date of the Clementines," 147–149; Schwartz, "Unzeitgemässe Beobachtungen," 178.
[74] Rius-Camps, "Las Pseudoclementinas," 79–158; Wehnert, "Abriss," 211–235; Cirillo, "L'écrit pseudo-clémentin," 223–237; Pouderon, "Aux origines," 21–48.

Recognitions "unconditionally" take priority, as Jones states?[75] Sergio Basso challenges this Lachmannian approach and the *Grundschrift* theory, proposing that the *Clementine* corpus be viewed as a body of distinct rhetorical instantiations, comparable to the notion of *canovacci* ("canvases") in Italian theatre. Narrative frameworks and fluid story bits circulated, rather than fully elaborated textual witnesses.[76] This shift emphasizes the *Clementines* as part of late-ancient literary fluidity. Similarly, Wehnert and Côté reject the idea of a single *Grundschrift*, highlighting the notion of multiple *Schichten* (layers) and *Stufen* (stages).[77] Hence, our focus on the manner in which the extant *Pseudo-Clementine* versions were composed and read in the fourth century.

Nevertheless, the extant versions still remain the subject of deconstruction into possible older sources of potential historical interest. An additional factor that has stimulated the "disentanglement" of the *Klementia* into older (Jewish-)Christian literary sources is the introductory writings, which provide an additional framework for the narrative. These letters, absent in the *Recognitions* (at least in Rufinus' version), have often been approached as separate, older sources not originally written by the *Klementinist*.[78] Ullmann views the *EpCl* not only as an earlier witness of apostolic succession, but also as a separate legal document concerning the papal legacy of Rome at the end of the second century.[79] Consequently, the letters are not regarded as coherent, nor even as part of the *Klementinist* narrative. Scholars such as Georg Strecker and François Bovon attribute the *EpPt* and *Adj* to the author of the hypothetical *KP*,[80] while Carl Schmidt and Stanley Jones argue that these letters (in particular *EpPt* and *D*) were written by the *Basic Writer*.[81] In a 2016 article concerning the *EpPt*, Matthew R. Crawford still suggests that the letter is to be isolated from the *Klementinist* narrative, which, thus, is not considered as a textual unity but rather fragmented into pieces which may have held a certain historical value.[82]

Another example commonly referred to is *Klem.* 4–6, the so-called *Apion section*, which is original to the *Klementinist* tradition.[83] In this

---

[75] Jones, "The Orphic Cosmo-Theogony," 72.
[76] Basso, "*Homilies*," 115.
[77] Wehnert, *Pseudoklementinische Homilien*, 30–36; Côté, *Pseudo-Clément*, 197.
[78] *Contra* Wehnert, "Literarkritik," 300.
[79] Ullmann, "The Significance of the Epistola Clementis," 295–317; Ullmann, "Some Remarks on the Significance," 331.
[80] Strecker, *Das Judenchristentum*, 137–138; Bovon, "En tête des Homélies," 335.
[81] Schmidt, *Studien*, 93; Jones, "Eros," 119.
[82] Crawford, "Κανών," 262.
[83] Cf. De Vos, "The Role," 54–88.

section, Clement, now a student of Peter, meets the grammarian and old acquaintance Appion (written with double "p" in the *Klementia*). Appion's character is based on the historical Apion, whom we know as a Homeric scholar and, above all, an anti-Jewish spokesman (cf. Flavius Josephus' *Contra Apionem*). Unlike the rest of the *Klementia*, this meeting does not discuss Scriptural hermeneutics, the role of the Evil One, or even Jesus as the True Prophet. Moreover, Peter himself plays no role in this meeting. Instead, Clement and Appion discuss the value of Greek *paideia*, including rhetorical education and philosophical traditions such as the interpretation of an Orphic Cosmogony. Hence, this passage was promptly considered a remnant of a separate, older source, as was first suggested by Adolf Hilgenfeld and subsequently by many others such as Hans Waitz, Werner Heintze, and Carl Schmidt, and even more recently by William Adler and James Carleton Paget.[84] The latter, for example, argues that the hypothetical source of *Klem.* 4–6 represents an "example of [Syriac] Jewish literature" from 115–150 AD. However, Pouderon believes the Apion disputes were an original creation by the *Grundschrift* author.[85]

Such a diachronic and *quellenkritische* reading has rendered the *Klementia* (as well as the *Grundschrift* and *Recognitions*) a patchwork of older, mostly hypothetical sources, overshadowing studies of its fourth-century context. This perspective has profoundly influenced views on the literary nature of the *Klementia*, considering it an assemblage redacted by a "compiler" rather than a unique late-ancient narrative of a skillful author.[86] John Chapman, in 1908, had already called for renewed appreciation of the *Klementia* as an original work situated within its fourth-century context.[87] However, only recently have scholars increasingly – albeit moderately – supported this call. Synchronic readings and reappraisals of the extant versions of the *Recognitions* and *Klementia* as distinct fourth-century narratives have, according to Bremmer, "still happened very rarely …, but this is evidently the future for the study of the *Clementines*."[88]

We shall not focus on (hypothetical) source-critical analyses, except where they shed light on the *Klementinist*'s editorial decisions and

---

[84] Hilgenfeld, *Die Clementinischen*, 224; Waitz, *Die Pseudoklementinen*, 251–256; Heintze, *Der Klemensroman*, 22–23; Schmidt, *Studien*, 298; Adler, "Apion's 'Encomium of Adultery'," 15–49; Carleton Paget, *Jews*, 427–492.
[85] Pouderon, "La genèse," 322.
[86] Cf. Jones, "Introduction to the *Pseudo-Clementines*," 31–34.
[87] Chapman, "On the Date of the Clementines," 155.
[88] Bremmer, "*Pseudo-Clementines*," 236–237.

literary engagement. Our focus is on the textual unity and purpose of the *Klementinist* narrative. Gershom Scholem saw the *Klementia* as a fourth-century "strange Jewish-Christian-Hellenistic hodge-podge" of early Jewish mystical traditions and Ebionite material, of interest only for its older sources.[89] I instead contest that the multifaceted character of the *Klementia* proves an invaluable factor which indicates the *Klementinist*'s active participation in a broader, social and intellectual dialogue characteristic of Late Antiquity, while reinterpreting earlier sources to serve his own purpose. The "self-isolated realm of specialist source-critical debate"[90] can hence be further shifted towards a synchronic reading and literary and historical study of its contemporary intellectual context.

Recent contributions, including those in the edited volumes of Amsler (together with Frey and Touati) and Bremmer,[91] have specifically considered the extant *Pseudo-Clementine* versions as distinct narratives within their fourth-century context. Scholars should recognize the unique narrative logic of the *Recognitions* and *Klementia*, avoiding the common methodological "temptation to harmonize" them, as Amsler has indicated.[92] This Element emphatically supports the shift towards approaching the *Klementia* as a unique work with its own textual unity, and advocates reading it as a late-ancient expression of Christian fiction which should be read in comparison to other expressions of novelistic prose. While harmonizing should be avoided, comparing the broader *Pseudo-Clementine* corpus and analyzing sources used in the construction of the *Klementia* (i.e., "redactive criticism"; as suggested by Kelley regarding the *Recognitions*[93]) can help identify the *Klementinist*'s distinct editorial choices when compared to other *Pseudo-Clementine* traditions. In particular, choices regarding fictional strategies and reflections on truth are fundamental in our approach to the *Klementia*. Having here established our approach of an "independent" and synchronic reading of the *Klementinist* narrative, a few words are necessary to briefly address earlier studies on the *Klementia*'s dating and sociocultural and intellectual context, before delving further into the *status* of the *Klementia* as fiction and the *Klementinist* as an original author.

---

[89] Scholem, *On the Kabbalah*, 172.
[90] Reed, "Reflections on F. Stanley Jones," 93.
[91] Amsler et al., *Nouvelles intrigues*; Bremmer, *The Pseudo-Clementines*.
[92] Amsler, "Peter," 178.
[93] Kelley, "On Recycling," 109.

The Fourth-Century *Klementinist*

Earlier scholarship defined the *Klementia* (and its relationship with the *Grundschrift* and *Recognitions*) in terms of "orthodoxy" and "unorthodoxy," placing it within "earliest Jewish-Christianity." Scholars considered the *Klementia* as a second- or early third-century text, written in an Ebionite circle reacting to Gnosis and Greek philosophy.[94] Other scholars, such as Gerhard Uhlhorn, considered the *Klementia* a second-century Jewish-Christian Gnostic writing.[95] Baur saw it as anti-Marcionite and Christian-Gnostic.[96] Hence, numerous scholars regarded the *Klementia* as reflecting an "unorthodox" or even a marginalized group, contrasting with "Catholic orthodoxy," as, for example, would be represented by the *Recognitions*. Charles Bigg, considering the *Klementia* as the product of a Catholic convert to Ebionism and "highly unorthodox editor," suggested the *Recognitions* represented "a recast in orthodox direction of the *Homilies*."[97] Later scholarship, however, re-evaluated the *Klementia*'s dating and historical significance with respect to the fourth-century religious landscape.

By the end of the nineteenth century, Baur's view of the *Klementia* as a second-century work was largely abandoned (except by Joseph Langen).[98] Most scholars concur nowadays with Bigg, who opted for a fourth-century dating, noting the presence of concepts such as *homoousios* (*Klem.* 20.7), fitting the fourth-century Christological, Trinitarian, and Arian debates.[99] Some scholars, such as Waitz, suggest the *Klementinist* was involved in Arian circles shortly after the Council of Nicaea,[100] while Bernhard Rehm believes the author was active before it.[101] Stanley Jones narrows the dating to 320–324, proposing that Eusebius' witness in his *Historia Ecclesiastica* 3.38.5 actually refers to the *Klementia*, with a *terminus ante quem* of 324 AD.[102]

---

[94] Neander, *Genetische Entwicklung*, 361, 368–370; Schliemann, *Die Clementinen*, 80, 326.
[95] Uhlhorn, *Die Homilien und Recognitionen*, 431.
[96] Baur, *Die christliche Gnosis*, 313, 400–405.
[97] Bigg, "The Clementine Homilies," 184 and 175.
[98] Baur, "Die Christuspartei," 405; Langen, *Die Klemensromane*, 21ff.
[99] Bigg, "The Clementine Homilies," 192.
[100] Waitz, *Die Pseudoklementinen*, 369.
[101] Rehm, "Zur Entstehung," 160.
[102] Jones, "Introduction to the *Pseudo-Clementines*," 38; *Contra*: According to Schwartz ("Unzeitgemässe Beobachtungen," 163 and 176), Eusebius is referring to the *Grundschrift*. However, as other scholars have argued, Eusebius' testimony is unclear (Carleton Paget, *Jews*, 440), since Eusebius mentions alleged disputes between Peter and Appion which are not found in the *Recognitions*, *Klementia*, or the Syriac *Pseudo-Clementines*.

The idea that the *Klementia* originated in Rome, as proposed by Baur,[103] remained the consensus until Uhlhorn (who still considered the *Klementia* a second-century text) suggested a Syrian provenance based on affinities with so-called Gnostic Jewish-Christianity.[104] A Syrian origin, absent the Gnostic notion, gained acceptance,[105] with scholars favoring the locations of Antioch on the Orontes (or Apamea, near Antioch), and Edessa. Moreover, recent focus on the early-fourth-century context of these areas has proven advantageous regarding further definition of the *Klementia*'s origin. Scholars such as Waitz, Chapman, Schwartz, Rehm, Côté, and Pouderon locate it within the culturally dynamic fourth-century Antioch, noting its Judaizing and/or Arian tendencies.[106] Already in 1932, Schwartz argued that the *Klementia*'s pro-Jewish reflections on self-identification as Ἰουδαῖος (*Ioudaios*) align with fourth-century debate within the Christian congregation of Antioch rather than being a remnant of second- and third-century "Jewish-Christian" material.[107] For example, the *Adversus Iudaeos* of the fourth-century bishop of Antioch, John Chrysostom, targeted Judaizing Christians. These latter observed Jewish rules and attended the synagogue. In the *Klementia*, Peter also emphasizes the observance of several purity laws and other rules known from the Scriptures (e.g., *Klem.* 7.8), and criticizes those who dare to argue that he would preach a dissolution of the Law (*EpPt* section 1.2). Hence, according to Jones, "[t]he author may belong among the Antiochene Judaizers."[108]

Other scholars, such as Bremmer and Kelley, with the latter also accepting Antioch as a possibility, suggest Edessa as the origin of the *Pseudo-Clementines*.[109] The discovery of the 411 Edessene manuscript (*British Library add. 12,150*) could point to an ongoing – if we consider the *Grundschrift* to be of Edessene origin – Edessene interest in the *Pseudo-Clementine* literature. It is also interesting to note that the eighth-century

---

[103] Baur, "Die Christuspartei," 405.
[104] Uhlhorn, *Die Homilien und Recognitionen*, 433.
[105] Cf. Bigg, "The Clementine Homilies," 169–170.
[106] Waitz, *Die Pseudoklementinen*, 369; Chapman, "On the Date of the Clementines," 154n1; Schwartz, "Unzeitgemässe Beobachtungen," 151–199; Rehm, "Clemens Romanus II," 199; Côté, "Les procédés rhétoriques," 204–210; Pouderon, "La genèse," 334. *Contra* the opinion that the *Klementinist* (concerning the idea of *homoousios*) was an Arian, see Lorenz (*Arius Judaizans?*, 153). Lorenz suggests the extension of Wisdom from the One God and the contraction of unity, as discussed in *Klem.* 16.12.1–2, refers to Marcellus of Ancyra, a proponent of the miahypostatic tradition.
[107] Schwartz, "Unzeitgemässe Beobachtungen," 163, 176; cf. also Vähäkangas, "Christian Identity," 231.
[108] Jones, "Introduction to the *Pseudo-Clementines*," 37.
[109] Bremmer, "*Pseudo-Clementines*," 236–249; Kelley, *Knowledge and Authority*, 182ff.

Nestorian Theodore bar Koni, hailing from East Syria, could still peruse a complete copy of the *Klementia*.[110] The Christian diversity in Edessa, including Arians and Judaizing Christians as described by Ephraem in 363 AD, bolsters the plausibility of this theory. However, as I discuss soon, I favor Antioch as origin.

A considerable amount of work has been conducted on late-ancient Jewish-Christian relations, particularly by Annette Yoshiko Reed, who examines the *Klementia* within a fourth-century context. She specifically explores how the *Klementia* defines its social–religious identity in relation to late-ancient Rabbinic traditions, and thus pays considerable attention to the nuances of the construction of "Judeo-Christianity," the theory of the "Parting of the Ways," and the *Klementia*'s role in scholarship of the history of Judaism and Christianity.[111] Moreover, as Reed has further demonstrated, the *Klementinist* narrative endeavors to present its own "orthodox" view on the relation between Jews and Christians and the true apostolic transmission of knowledge, and the path to salvation, within a fourth-century context.[112]

The *Klementia* has also often been considered anti-Marcionite and/or anti-Appelean, views still relevant to the fourth century.[113] Another emerging focus is its potential role as a fourth-century reaction against Gnostic traditions.[114] Attention to its contemporary context has led to a renewed and original focus on then contemporary Judaizing Christian relations, Rabbinic Judaism, Gnostic traditions, and anti-Marcionism within a heresiological framework. This *Klementinist*'s self-identification as Ἰουδαῖος [*Ioudaios*] and the additional doctrine of *syzygies* emphasize the effort to assert a claim to truth. According to this theory, the world is divided into two parts, a good and bad king, a true and false line of prophecy, true and false *gnosis*, and two opposing religious identities, as Peter states in *Klem.* 11.16.2–4:

> For he is a worshipper of God (θεοσεβὴς), ..., who is truly pious, not one who is such only in name, but who really performs the deeds of the law (νόμου ... τὰς πράξεις) that has been given him. If anyone acts impiously, he is not pious; in like manner as, if he who is of another tribe keeps the law, he is a Jew (Ἰουδαῖός); but he who does not keep it is a Greek (Ἕλλην). For the Jew believes God and keeps the law, by which faith he removes also other sufferings, though like mountains and heavy.[115]

---

[110] Nöldeke, "Bar Choni," 501–507; Bremmer, "*Pseudo-Clementines*," 240–241.
[111] Cf. Reed, *Jewish-Christianity*, 217–253.
[112] Reed, "'Jewish Christianity'," 189–231.
[113] Cf. Kelley, *Knowledge and Authority*, 187–189; Le Boulluec, "La *Monarchia*," 437–450.
[114] Regarding the *Klementia*: Therrien, *Gnose*; regarding the *Recognitions*: Amsler, "Peter," 186; regarding the *Grundschrift*: Bazzana, "Eve," 313–320.
[115] Roberts and Donaldson, *Ante-Nicene Christian Library Vol. XVII*, 181; Rehm and Strecker, *Die Pseudoklementinen I*, 162.

While Jones argues that the *Basic Writer* identifies with the third group of the θεοσεβεῖς (*theosebeis*),[116] distinct from "Jews" and "Greeks," it is clear that the *Klementinist* employs a different strategy of self-identification of "Jews" rather than "Greeks." There is no strong "Christian" supersessionist attitude towards Jews. The self-identification of the "Jew" forms a more flexible category in an inclusive and apologetic perspective,[117] encompassing Christ-following Jews and non-Christ-following Jews, since Jesus is considered as a True Prophet in line with Moses and offering the same teachings.

Recent studies focus on how the *Klementinist* positions himself within contemporary religious discussions and self-identifies within the work. Another key aspect of the *Klementinist* and the way in which he presents himself that has come to the fore in recent years is as *pepaideumenos* and his interaction with Greek *paideia*, including rhetoric, philosophy, and literature. The narrative indicates a negative reception of Greek culture, depicting "Greeks," particularly philosophers, as eristic *philologoi* rather than truth-loving *philosophoi* (cf. *Klem.* 1.10). However, I contend that the *Klementinist* seeks to express a clear voice in the debate concerning philosophy, rhetoric, and *paideia* as someone who, clearly in his capacity as *pepaideumenos*, reflects on Christian *paideia* and the relation to literature and fiction. This view is essential to recognizing the *Klementinist* as an original author and the *Klementia* as unique Christian fiction.

Klementinist Pepaideumenos

Greek *paideia* is fiercely criticized in the *Klementia* (cf. *Klem.* 4.12.1), a concern echoed by Ephraem of Nisibis' scathing critique of Greek *paideia* in Edessa, which he labelled "venomous,"[118] and by John Chrysostom's sharp critique of *paideia* in Antioch, a late-ancient city of power and *paideia*.[119] Regarding the *Klementia*'s origin, I here note that not Edessa but Antioch plays a fundamentally symbolic role in the *Klementia*. At the narrative's end, when Peter, Clement, and his family journey towards Antioch, the city represents a Christian *lieu de mémoire* – just as it is symbolic that Clement's journey began in Rome and detoured via Alexandria: these three places represent centers of worldly and cultural power and, thus, ideal places for *pepaideumenoi* such as Clement, Nicetas, Appion, and Simon. Clement seeks to escape the epistemological *vanitas* of magicians

---

[116] Jones, "Jewish Christianity," 138–151.
[117] Hogeterp, "Judaism and Hellenism," 59–71; Duncan, *Novel Hermeneutics*, 15.
[118] Cf. Kelley, *Knowledge and Authority*, 199.
[119] Cf. Wilken, *John Chrysostom*.

and Rome's philosophers and confronts Alexandria's philosophers with their eristic, non-truth-loving attitudes. Antioch represents the location where the *gentile* people will ultimately be won over by Peter, and where Simon will be driven away.

However, this critique of *paideia* is not a simple rejection, as the *Klementia* itself is a product of this same *paideia*. The *Klementinist*, as *pepaideumenos*, actively engages in debates regarding cultural identity, philosophy, rhetoric, in addition to conducting meta-literary reflections as to what it entails to write and read Greek literature. In 1908, John Chapman stated that the authors of the various *Pseudo-Clementine* versions were post-Nicene and that the *Recognitions* (ca. 365–380) refuted the version of the Arian *Klementinist*.[120] With respect to my own aims, it is particularly interesting that he also suggested that the "Pseudo-Clement" was "perhaps a former sophist" and "convert from heathenism to the Imperial religion."[121] Chapman thus not only emphasized the Arian character of the *Klementinist*, but he also underscored the latter's relation to Greek *paideia* as a former Sophist, while minimizing other possible factors of the author's social identity: "there is no reason to think he was a Judæo-Christian, an Elchasaïte, or anti-Pauline, or anti-Marcionite, that he employed ancient sources, that he belonged to a secretive sect."[122] Chapman regarded the *Pseudo-Clementines* as a response, written between 360 and 410 AD, to the resurgence of Neoplatonic philosophy, polytheism, and theurgy promoted by Emperor Julian. Compared to other scholars, Chapman's views were and still remain both original and thought-provoking.

Recent insight into the *Grundschrift* and *Klementia* provide nuance to Chapman's view on their post-Nicene dating and the supposed absence of an anti-Marcionite stance. I contend that Chapman's approach to the social and cultural identity of the "Pseudo-Clement," however, as an ex-Sophist merits reconsideration, since I argue that we are not dealing with – as Chapman stated – an "ex-sophist" who aims to refute Greek *paideia*, but rather, with an author who consciously reflects on and reconsiders the cultural capital of *paideia* by means of reflections on novelistic narrative tradition, encouraging readers to reconsider their own status as *pepaideumenoi*, the redefined aspects of Christian *paideia*, and, particularly, what it means to read literature as a *pepaideumenos*.

The definition of *paideia* and the social identity of late-ancient *pepaideumenoi* have been studied in depth by scholars like Werner Jaeger,

---

[120] Chapman, "On the Date of the Clementines," 25–26; Chapman, "Clementines," 39–44.
[121] Chapman, "On the Date of the Clementines," 155.
[122] Chapman, "Clementines."

Henri-Irénée Marrou, Graham Anderson, Peter Brown, Sara Rappe, and Kendra Eshleman.[123] Chapman's view of the *Klementinist* as a converted ex-Sophist demands reconsideration, as the social identities of Sophists, *pepaideumenoi*, and Christians are not mutually exclusive. The role of *paideia*, as a pervasive form of cultural capital, among the late-ancient educated elite cannot be overstated and is closely connected to negotiating identity, particularly the distinct "Greek" and "Christian" identities.[124] Arthur Urbano defines *paideia* as the elite's "habitus," a concept introduced by Pierre Bourdieu,[125] implying a complex set of ideas and practices that translate into cultural authority and prestige:

> ... interactions among Christian and non-Christian elite in the Greek-speaking contexts of the late Roman empire are better understood as debates and exchanges within a segment of society that was occupied with the negotiation of identity, specifically, what it meant to be a "Greek," or a "Christian," and what the shifting landscapes of late antiquity meant for the Greek intellectual and literary heritage. Christians were not "cultural outsiders."[126]

The *Klementia* reveals *Iudaioi* as cultural insiders, particularly through its philosophical discussions. While Chapman suggested first a *Clementine* refutation of Neoplatonic philosophers lurking behind the *persona* of Simon Magus (without offering further elaboration),[127] it is only recently that Neoplatonic and Neopythagorean interests have been recognized as fruitful for comparison. In this stead, Dominique Côté has raised insightful discussion regarding the role of the Orphic Cosmogony in the *Pseudo-Clementines* in dialogue with fourth-century Neoplatonism.[128] Côté also explores Simon's original characterization in the *Klementia* in relation to Neoplatonic discussions concerning theurgy and intellectual contemplation.[129]

It is in this regard that Côté describes the *Klementinist* as part of "a writing and thinking elite, given his education and religion. Culturally, he is a Greek because of his education, not his religion. He seeks to define

---

[123] Jaeger, *Paideia*; Marrou, *Histoire de l'éducation*, 151–160; Anderson, "The Pepaideumenos," 79–208; Brown, *Power and Persuasion*, 35–70; Rappe, "The New Math," 405–432; Eshleman, *The Social World*, 21–90.
[124] Cf. Ehrenkrook, "Christians, Pagans," 255–265.
[125] Bourdieu, *Les règles*, 292–297.
[126] Urbano, *The Philosophical Life*, 8.
[127] Chapman, "On the Date of the Clementines," 157.
[128] Côté, "La théogonie orphique," 85–122.
[129] Côté, "Simon Magus," 261–301.

himself in relation to the παιδεία."¹³⁰ As Côté argues, the *Klementia* should be considered *historical fiction* or "un roman historique," namely a narrative set in the first century, which, moreover, reflects *paideutic* involvement in the fourth century.¹³¹ This aspect is significant for fiction, as various strategies deployed throughout the *Klementia* encourage the *pepaideumenos* to contemplate these philosophical themes and recognize how the *Klementinist* takes positions in relation to Neoplatonic philosophers by means of a shared *paideutic* background.

That notion of *paideia* is embedded in the entire rhetoric of the work. Meinolf Vielberg addresses the literary and rhetorical techniques used by the *Klementinist* to weave a narrative world replete with tensions between *pepaideumenoi*.¹³² Opponents such as Simon Magus, Appion the grammarian, Athenodorus the Epicurean, and Annubion the astrologer, as well as protagonists such as Clement (explicitly) and Peter (implicitly), remarkably embody the essence of Greek *paideia*, all capable of sophisticated rhetorical and philosophical debate.

Peter, for example, represents a philosopher able to engage in sophisticated discussion, in more elaborate fashion than in the other *Pseudo-Clementine* traditions.¹³³ He offers original theories on the *unde malum*-question (*Klem.* 19 and 20), revelatory truth (*Klem.* 17.13–20), and the divine (e.g., *Klem.* 17.1–12), which can be best approached in a Neoplatonic context. Peter's opponents are characterized as eristic Sophists, and, remarkably, the *Klementinist* even makes use of references to Plato's oeuvre regarding the way in which Sophists are characterized. In this respect, Simon Magus is presented as Simon the Sophist, while Appion, in regard to his rhetorical–philosophical abilities, resembles Plato's Phaedrus from the eponymous dialogue and the *Symposium*.¹³⁴

This observation sheds light on the originality of the *Klementia* as Christian fiction: not only is it "historical fiction," which also engages with various contemporary fourth-century intellectual debates, but it, moreover, features ongoing literary dialogue with Platonic dialogues. Simon Magus and Appion are portrayed as Sophists in Platonic fashion, while Peter is a true philosopher confronting their sophistry. As I recently discussed, the *Klementia* also reflects on the Platonic discourse of myth at a meta-discursive

---

[130] Côté, "Simon Magus," 299.
[131] Côté, *Le thème de l'opposition*, 111–261.
[132] Vielberg, "Rhetoric in the Ancient and Christian Novel," 145–162.
[133] De Vos, "The Literary Characterisation of Peter," 483–509.
[134] De Vos, "Plato's Phaedrus and Symposium in the Pseudo-Clementine Homilies," 102–146.

level.[135] For example, the Myth of Er (*Republic* 614–621) functions as a hypotext in the passage of Faustus, Clement's father, who queries the consequences of the life choices one has made (*Klem.* 15.5–8). The choice of the Myth of Er as hypotext prompts reflection on righteous living, providence, and the role of philosophy versus prophecy. In the *Republic*, Socrates calls Er's story a myth through which we might be "saved" (ἡμᾶς ἂν σώσειεν; 621b), urging reflection on life choices and their consequences. For Socrates, this myth serves as a significant strategy for addressing the concept of truth in regard to the reader/audience. By incorporating this myth as hypotext, the *Klementinist* also explores the discourse regarding Platonic myth and the assertions towards truth that go with it: the reader is expected to recognize the hypotextual Myth of Er, and, moreover, the author seeks to demonstrate that the truth is revealed through the conversion story of Faustus and Peter's interpretation of his life. Thus, the *Klementia,* as a work of Christian fiction, seeks to articulate a literary–philosophical discourse on truth that surpasses the myths and dialogues of Plato.

The *Klementia* as Original Greek Novelistic Prose?

The *Klementinist* was evidently aware of the literary and fictional strategies within his work and the different dynamics of truth and belief. I shall focus on another aspect of the fictional strategies of this work: its interaction with Greek erotic novelistic prose such as Chariton's *Chaereas and Callirhoe* and Achilles Tatius' *Leucippe and Cleitophon*. The *Klementinist* engages with these expressions of novelistic fiction, and with the tradition of Greek erotic prose in general, to offer an original reflection on *paideia* and to examine what it means to read and write novelistic fiction as a *pepaideumenos*. In other words, what dynamics shape the relationship between reading and writing fiction and the identity formation of a Christian *pepaideumenos*? Reflections on *paideia* are central here, particularly in the form of hypertextual connections with and meta-literary reflections on the Greek novelistic prose fiction of Chariton and Achilles Tatius. The analysis of these connections will show that the *Klementinist* considers the status of Christian fiction, reading strategies, and cultural identity in relation to the act of writing and reading fiction. I would hence like to address, by discussing the *Klementia* in relation to Greek erotic prose, a comment by Stanley Jones: "Further study of this literary environment will doubtless illuminate the author [BDV: the *Klementinist*]'s achievements."[136]

---

[135] De Vos, "Living Philosophical Fiction," 53–84.
[136] Jones, "Introduction to the *Pseudo-Clementines*," 37.

Nevertheless, as mentioned earlier, the literary qualities of the *Klementia* have been greatly ignored. This point can particularly be noted in recent *Companions* and handbooks on ancient narrative and fiction. Edwards noted that the *Pseudo-Clementines*:

> ... are treated all too frequently as material for historians, not for critics. A book on the ancient novel is sufficiently erudite if the author shows that he has read them; the *Homilies* are omitted in a volume of translations under the title of *Collected Ancient Greek Novels*.[137] It might be said that this is as it should be, since the *Homilies* are largely what their title advertises, and even the *Recognitions* contain much that is extrinsic to the plot. By itself (it might be said) this threadbare plot holds little to engage us, and is disposed of in a few pages in the works of Hägg[138] and Perry.[139] ... this neglect is undeserved.[140]

Thirty years later, the *Pseudo-Clementines* remain overlooked in general works on ancient narrative. The *Cambridge Companion to the Greek and Roman Novel* only mentions thrice the *Recognitions* (not the *Klementia*), based on Pervo's negative evaluation.[141] The *Blackwell Companion to Late Antique Literature* refers twice to the *Pseudo-Clementines* and its anti-Pauline and possible Arian character.[142] In recent years, increased scholarly attention has been devoted to the relationship between "pagan" ancient fiction and early Christian and Jewish narratives, such as Apocryphal Acts, *Vitae*, *Passiones*, and so-called fringe novels like *Josaphat and Barlaam*. In these studies, too, the *Pseudo-Clementine* versions remain neglected, as in the volume *Ancient Fiction: The Matrix of Early Christian and Jewish Narrative*,[143] or are only minimally discussed, as in *The Ancient Novel and Early Christian and Jewish Narrative: Fictional Intersections*.[144] Edwards' remark on the neglected status of the *Pseudo-Clementines* hence remains highly poignant.

Defining the genre of the ancient novel, not to mention the concept of ancient fiction itself, is already challenging.[145] While Edwards approaches the *Pseudo-Clementine* corpus as "a Christian response to

---

[137] Reardon, *Collected Ancient Greek Novels*.
[138] Hägg, *The Novel*, 154–165.
[139] Perry, *The Ancient Romances*, 285–293.
[140] Edwards, "The *Clementina*," 459.
[141] Whitmarsh, *The Cambridge Companion*, 13, 107n50, 192.
[142] McGill and Watts, *A Companion to Late Antique Literature*, 408, 410.
[143] Brant et al., *Ancient Fiction*.
[144] Pinheiro et al., *The Ancient Novel*, 43n41, 111, 113, 120.
[145] Cf. Morgan, "Make Believe;" Messis, "Fiction," 313–342; De Temmerman, "Ancient Biography," 3–25.

the pagan novel,"[146] István Czachesz considers it ancient biographical literature, arguing it cannot be termed an ancient novel.[147] Since the late nineteenth century, however, a majority of scholars has agreed that the *Pseudo-Clementines* should be considered a novel, as Erwin Rohde stated.[148] The latter regarded the *Pseudo-Clementines* as a Christian narrative incorporating the schema of pagan adventure novels. This, however, has not been the prevailing view in subsequent studies. Most scholars, particularly those focusing entirely on the *Pseudo-Clementines*, have considered the work to be a novel, albeit not an original one, as the *Grundschrift* author would have clumsily adopted and adapted the framework of another, non-Christian novel. This negative perception was already expressed by Charles Bigg: (As regards composition, let us observe that the work, though cast in dramatic form, exhibits not the least vestige of dramatic ability. The characters are merely wooden puppets, left lying in a corner until they are wanted, and then shuffled awkwardly on to the stage. Personality they have none).[149]

Wilhelm Bousset argued that the *Grundschrift* author made several mistakes in reworking the original novel, which remained unnoticed by the *Klementinist* and *Recognitionist*.[150] Among other things, Bousset pointed out the lack of psychological motivation as to why Mattidia, Clement's as-of-yet unrecognized mother, chooses to consciously deceive Peter. When Peter queries her, a beggar at the gate of a temple in Aradus, about her misfortunes, she claims her lost husband is a Sicilian, not a Roman (*Klem.* 12.19.4). Bousset also criticized the unrealistic distance of Aradus from Athens, Mattidia's intended destination. Additionally, the real, similar names of the twins Nicetas and Aquila, namely Faustinus and Faustinianus, do not hold any function as a literary *topos*, as is the case with similar sounding names in other ancient narratives. Moreover, Bousset suggested that the original Greek novel featured the twin theme, which the later *Pseudo-Clementine* author expanded by adding a third son, Clement.[151] Noteworthy, twelve years later, Bousset offered an alternative view: rather than being a Greek novel, he argued that the source of the *Basic Writing* was instead of Hellenistic-Jewish origin, based on the

---

[146] Edwards, "The *Clementina*," 459.
[147] Czachesz, "The Clement Romance," 24–35.
[148] Rohde, *Der griechische Roman*, 507.
[149] Bigg, "The Clementine Homilies," 160.
[150] Bousset, "Die Wiedererkennungs-Fabel," 27; see also Heintze (*Der Klemensroman*, 10), who refers to "Spuren einer höchst nachlässigen Komposition."
[151] Bousset, "Die Wiedererkennungs-Fabel," 26–27.

motifs of familial love and a brother-in-law's accusation, as can also be found within the later *Thousand and One Nights*.[152]

However, in the meantime, Bousset's initial view had been adopted by Heintze, who argued that Clement's failure to hug his brothers upon recognition (*Klem.* 13.3) represented a literary inconsistency from a psychological point of view.[153] This negative perception of the literary qualities of the *Pseudo-Clementine* redactors was reinforced by attempts to identify a pagan, anti-astrological novelistic *Quelle*,[154] diverting attention from the works in their current form. This theory of an original pagan novel underlying the *Pseudo-Clementines* has since persisted.[155] The suggested use of a pagan novel is often attributed to its entertainment value. This is the so-called *coattail theory*, according to which Christian authors capitalized on the popularity of novelistic prose.[156] While the novel, or at least the motif of the recognitions, may have rendered the content more appealing, numerous scholars in the fields both of history of religion and of literary studies ultimately argue its irrelevance to the theological–philosophical debates present in the *Pseudo-Clementine* versions.

The *Klementia* has commonly been read as an apologetic work, even as a work intended to convert gentiles [*Bekehrungsschrift*], with the narrative framework of recognitions considered "superfluous" and having no function other than rendering the doctrines more attractive to read,[157] and thus to edify "non-Christian" readers.[158] An additional view along this vein which particularly concerns the *Grundschrift* is that the work serves an apologetic purpose in educating catechumens,[159] or aiding "Christian missionaries in their encounters with pagan philosophers."[160] The *Pseudo-Clementine* traditions are thus viewed as heresiological, with

---

[152] Bousset, "Die Geschichte eines Wiedererkennungsmärchens," 533–534.
[153] Heintze, *Der Klemensroman*, 116–118.
[154] Cf. Heintze, *Der Klemensroman*, 134, 138; Cullmann, *Le problème littéraire et historique du roman pseudo-clémentin*, 119–121, 134ff.
[155] E.g., Trenkner, *The Greek Novella*, 101; Salač, "Die Pseudoklementinen," 45–49; Hägg, *The Novel*, 162–163; Holzberg, *The Ancient Novel*, 22–26; Perry (*The Ancient Romances*, 285–286 and 295) states that the *Grundschrift* and the *Historia Apollonii regis Tyri* have used the same source, based on the shared motif of family separation (rather than of a couple). According to Vielberg (*Klemens*, 143–144), there would have been indirect influence of the *Historia Apollonii regis Tyri* on the *Grundschrift* (see also Montiglio, *Love and Providence*, 213–214).
[156] E.g., Holzberg, *The Ancient Novel*, 22–23.
[157] Perry, *The Ancient Romances*, 291.
[158] Trenkner, *The Greek Novella*, 101; Hägg, *The Novel*, 164.
[159] Waitz, *Die Pseudoklementinen*, 48, 50.
[160] Teeple, *The Prophet in the Clementines*, 25.

the narrative framework (based on an older novel) serving apologetic purposes as part of a straightforward religious *Kulturkampf*.

"Ce n'était pas un sot!" ("He Was Not a Fool")

In recent years, however, the notion of a narrative framework of recognition scenes as merely a vestige of an older, novelistic source has been challenged, a development that also has implications for our understanding of the *Klementia*'s status as prose fiction. Shortly after Bousset, Karl Kerényi argued against the view that a Greek novel served as the framework for the *Pseudo-Clementines*. In his view, an unknown Christian author had written an original narrative, incorporating several motifs strongly present in Greek novels, to ultimately create a family romance. Kerényi, however, suggested the story was influenced by the Egyptian Isis-cult, specifically drawing parallels between Mattidia escaping from her brother-in-law and Isis fleeing from her mythical brother-in-law Seth, travelling to Byblos in search of her husband Osiris.[161] This religious story, then, would have been rearranged by the *Basic Writer*, who would have introduced an anti-astrological stance through means of Heliodorus' novel. This thesis of indirect religious influence was further developed by Reinhold Merkelbach in relation to a vast body of ancient novels, but remains unpopular among specialists in ancient narrative.[162]

Despite this, recent years have observed a moderately positive appreciation of the *Pseudo-Clementines* versions as unique narratives, though focus still centers on the *Grundschrift*. It bears repeating, however, that this view has yet to be fully reflected in general studies of ancient fiction, where the idea of a particular non-Christian novel as an original model persists. Scholars such as Bernhard Rehm, Mark J. Edwards, Paolo Liverani, Dirk Uwe Hansen, and, chiefly, F. Stanley Jones, in turn argue against the necessity of assuming a non-Christian source, shifting attention to the *Pseudo-Clementine* narrative's inherent literary qualities, be it with a strong emphasis on the hypothetical *Grundschrift*.[163]

Antoine Salles argues that "le compilateur qui a écrit le *Roman clémentin* [BDV: Salles' name for the *Grundschrift*] en utilisant des livres plus anciens, n'était pas précisément un écrivain classique, soucieux de surveiller son

---

[161] Kerényi, *Die griechisch-orientalische Romanliteratur*, 76–78, 93.
[162] Merkelbach, *Roman*, 172–177.
[163] Rehm, "Bardesanes," 218–247; Edwards, *The Clementina*, 459–474; Liverani, "Pietro Turista," 136–145; Hansen, "Die Metamorphose," 120 and 125; Jones, "Introduction," 26–27.

style et sa rédaction; mais ce n'était pas un sot" ("the compiler who wrote the *Clementine novel* using older books was not exactly a classical writer, concerned with carefully monitoring his style and composition; but he was not a fool").[164] However, Salles contends that the *Klementinist* and *Recognitionist* versions lack the quality of the *Grundschrift*, with discrepancies attributed to the later redactors (*remanieurs*).[165] Similarly, Jones praises the *Basic Writer* as "a very creative author, the one who wrote the first (and last) Christian novel, and by no means a paltry one – the one at the root of the entire Western Faust saga."[166] This raises the question, viewing the *Pseudo-Clementines* as an original Christian novel, as to how, in this case, the *Basic Writer* interacted with Greek novelists like Chariton, Achilles Tatius, and Heliodorus. For example, Hansen suggests he was familiar with Heliodorus' *Aethiopica* and responded to it by creating a new Christian hero.[167]

While the *Pseudo-Clementines* should indeed be considered an original work of prose fiction, one must heed the difficulties implied with respect to the denomination of "novel," bearing in mind Czachesz' criticism and the fact that there was no ancient genre of the novel.[168] In this regard, I am also cautious about labelling the *Klementia*, or the *Pseudo-Clementines* in general, simply as "a novel." However, I do wish to delve deeper into how the *Klementia*, in particular, interacts with expressions of so-called Greek novels and motifs that are distinctly developed in these texts, specifically those of Chariton, Achilles Tatius, Longus, Xenophon, and Heliodorus, and how this Christian prose creates an original meta-literary discourse reflecting on those novelistic motifs, evoking accompanying reflections on fiction.

Similar debates on whether or not a Christian expression of fiction is to be regarded as a novel can be observed regarding the *Apocryphal Acts of the Apostles* and pre- and post-Constantinian hagiographical narratives, which have received more nuanced attention in recent years than the *Pseudo-Clementine* literature, where the *coattail* still remains popular.[169] In 1991, Averil Cameron considered early Christian fiction as

---

[164] Salles, "Simon le magicien," 221.
[165] Salles, "Simon le magicien," 221–222.
[166] Jones, "The Genesis of Pseudo-Clementine Christianity," 204.
[167] Nowadays, Heliodorus' *Aethiopica* is dated to the second half of the fourth century (see De Temmerman, *Crafting Characters*, 2n4), which was not yet accepted by Hansen. Also Kerényi (*Die griechisch-orientalische Romanliteratur*, 78) had argued the use of Heliodorus (besides Chariton and Xenophon) by the third-century *Basic Writer* (see in the same line: Bremmer, "Achilles Tatius," 27).
[168] Czachesz, "The Clement Romance," 24–35.
[169] E.g., Pinheiro et al., *The Ancient Novel*; Bossu, "Steadfast and Shrewd Heroines," 91–128; Van Pelt et al., *Narrative, Imagination, and Concepts of Fiction*.

essentially different from erotic novelistic prose "in the matter of its relation to truth,"[170] emphasizing its protreptic nature. In a similar line, Jason König argued that apostle stories subvert expected elements of novelistic expression in order to highlight the narrative's Christian identity.[171] Subsequently, Glenn Snyder suggested that the *Apocryphal Acts of the Apostles* should not be classified as novels solely because they use themes and motifs from ancient novels.[172] Rather, these *Acts* demonstrate a creative application of the highly flexible novelistic modus.[173]

Recent scholarship focusing on the *Pseudo-Clementines* has explored in depth several literary motifs in the hypothetical *Grundschrift* (derived from a harmonized reading of the *Recognitions* and *Klementia*), particularly the "anagnorismos" or recognition motif. While recent scholarship has still considered the recognition motif as a mere "novelistic embellishment," Pascal Boulhol's analysis revealed how the motif – already going back to Homer's epics – is adapted to the *Grundschrift*'s theological and didactic goals, emphasizing the notion of divine providence.[174] János Bolyki also interpreted the theological act of recognition of others and oneself as metaphorical for the recognition of God, "organically" linking the recognition motif to the *Grundschrift*'s doctrinal themes.[175] Thus, the *Basic Writer* produced original philosophical–religious prose. But the question remains as to how to approach the extant versions as original Christian prose?

Over the past two decades, the *Recognitions* as an independent narrative has received limited scholarly attention compared to the *Grundschrift*. Meinolf Vielberg examined the literary and rhetorical dynamics which render the *Recognitions* a well-constructed *Bildungsroman*,[176] and Dominique Côté systematically analyzed the theme of opposition between Peter and Simon and compared it to other late-ancient narratives and literary Neopythagorean models such as those of Apollonius of Tyana in Philostratus' *Vita Apollonii* or Alexander of Abonoteichus in Lucian's eponymous work.[177] In 2006, Nicole Kelley offered an examination of the *Recognitions*' active engagement with fourth-century philosophy and astrology,[178] also comparing the *Recognitionist*'s own choices to the

---

[170] Cameron, *Christianity*, 117–119.
[171] König, "Novelistic and Anti-Novelistic Narrative," 121–149.
[172] Snyder, *Acts of Paul*, 112–120.
[173] Pervo, "The Ancient Novel," 686.
[174] Boulhol, "La conversion de l'anagnorismos profane," 151–175.
[175] Bolyki, "Recognitions in the *Pseudo-Clementina*," 199.
[176] Vielberg, *Klemens*.
[177] Côté, *Le thème de l'opposition*, 111ff.
[178] Kelly, *Knowledge and Authority*; see also Kelley, "Astrology," 607–629.

Grundschrift. For instance, the *Recognitionist* most likely did not share his predecessor's belief in fate's power over the unbaptized, a perspective that the *Basic Writer* seems to have adopted from Bardaisan.

Similar studies of the *Klementia* are both needed and desired. While the *Recognitions* have garnered moderate attention, a holistic approach to the *Klementinist* narrative has proven challenging theologically,[179] and also literary–philosophically. Numerous scholars have suggested that the *Klementia* exhibits little narrative unity and lacks a well-structured intellectual and moral development of Clement, as well as a clear progression of Peter's teachings throughout the narrative.[180]

Nevertheless, the *Klementia* merits approach as a well-constructed narrative, since, I argue, it provides original meta-reflective insight into the novelistic tradition, blending reflections on cultural identity and *paideutic* readership. I here nuance Jones' view of the *Grundschrift* as the "first (and last) Christian novel,"[181] bearing in mind the difficulty regarding the denomination of the "novel," as well as arguing that the extant *Pseudo-Clementine* versions, in particular the *Klementia*, offer distinct unique expressions of fiction and reflections on Greek erotic prose.

Hermeneutics and the Unity of the *Klementia*

An important initial step towards understanding the *Klementia*'s unity was made by Patricia Duncan, who considers the hermeneutics of reading and the interpretation of texts, such as the Scriptures and Gospels, as key to the narrative's structure: "Along the way, she [the reader] will have been trained – sometimes explicitly, sometimes by implication only – to read a variety of other literatures with new eyes."[182] The reader must engage with explicit discussions between Peter and Simon on the correct interpretation of the Scriptures, as well as with sometimes implicit reinterpretations of passages from the Gospels (or "Neu-Inszenierungen," as Tobias Nicklas calls them[183]) woven into the *Klementinist* narrative itself.

The *Klementinist*, to a far greater extent than the *Recognitions* and the hypothetical *Grundschrift*, emphasizes the correct hermeneutics of storytelling. Regarding the Scriptures, the *Klementinist* states that false pericopes intruded into the written Mosaic Law (e.g., *Klem.* 2.52), which was initially an oral and uncorrupted tradition, but became

---

[179] Cf. Jones, "A History of Research" (2012), 88.
[180] Cf. Vielberg, *Klemens*, 188; Stanton, "Jewish Christian Elements," 309.
[181] Jones, "The Genesis of Pseudo-Clementine Christianity," 204.
[182] Duncan, *Novel Hermeneutics*, 38.
[183] Nicklas, "Apocryphal Jesus," 131–145.

corrupted upon transcription (*Klem.* 2.38). Remarkably, according to the *Klementinist*, this transpired with God's approval. As illustrated in several elaborate discussions between Peter and Simon in *Klem.* 2 and 3, the audience's moral character is tested when reading or listening to these false pericopes. Those who accept negative assertions about Abraham, Moses, or God risk losing the image of God within their souls.[184] Thus, reading is presented as an act of good faith and an existential endeavor. Additionally, the potential for allegorical interpretation of texts is strongly refuted.[185] Thus, we are here dealing with Christian fiction that focuses on correct hermeneutics. In this context, Duncan refers to the *Klementia* as "revisionist historical fiction."[186]

This holds true, I argue, for Plato's dialogues. As previously mentioned, Plato's Myth of Er serves as a hypotext in the discussions between Faust and Peter, while the *Symposium* and the *Phaedrus* also play a significant, original role in the *Klementia*, which the reader must recognize and interpret appropriately within the context of *Klementinist* fiction.[187] In fact, the *Klementia* should also be regarded as philosophical fiction, or fiction that emphasizes philosophical reading and interpretation, with philosophical hermeneutics serving as an overarching unifying thread throughout. Thus, the *Klementia* is structured around three key Platonic pillars as the philosophical spine of the narrative:[188] 1) the Platonic pattern of true vision and noetic contemplation of God; 2) combined with the philosophical theme of images and their model (specifically the Platonizing lecture of *Gen.* 1:26–27); and 3) the Platonic theme of striving to become as closely like God as possible. This philosophical framework is intricately structured around Clement's contemplative journey, guided by the teachings of Peter, who is portrayed as modified Platonic philosopher through both explicit and implicit references to Platonic dialogues. The *Klementia* thus integrates Platonic philosophy to support its Christian philosophical message, and serves, as I argue, to complement Old and New Testament texts

---

[184] De Vos, "The Pseudo-Clementine Homilies and the Art of 'Fake News'," 423–459.
[185] Chapman ("On the Date of the Clementines," 154 and 154n1), with respect to his view that the *Klementia* were written in mid-fourth century Antioch, also referred to the so-called late-ancient "Antiochene School" and their "literal" and "typological" interpretation of the Scriptures. In that school, allegories and allegorical interpretations were often refuted, a point that remains important within the *Klementia* (Simon Magus is said to have deceived people by means of allegorical interpretations of the Scriptures and Greek myths, cf. *Klem.* 2.22.6; 2.25.3); for a more substantial discussion, see Shuve (*The Pseudo-Clementine Homilies*) and Carlson (*Jewish-Christian Interpretation*, 22).
[186] Duncan, *Novel Hermeneutics*, 26.
[187] Cf. De Vos, "Living Philosophical Fiction," 53–84.
[188] As is discussed in detail in De Vos, "From the Dark Platonic Cave," 221–260.

as hermeneutical lenses. This is evident in another Platonizing aspect of the *Klementia*: the concern about the dangers of written texts. Writing down the oral teachings of Moses and Jesus risks placing them beyond the control of their teachers. This explains why the written Torah contains false pericopes and why Peter warns that reading his doctrines without proper oral guidance could "numb" the reader (*EpPt* section 1.3). Thus, strict control over the written transmission of his teachings is necessary; in this case, his teachings as written down by Clement in the *Klementia*. This prompts a meta-narrative reflection on the *Klementia* itself. The dangers of reading without oral assistance and the correct philosophical guidance are also explored in *Klem.* 4–6, particularly in the reception of the *Phaedrus*, with its reflections on the perils of written texts,[189] the *erotikoi logoi* of Phaedrus and Socrates, the role of correct philosophical–rhetorical order, and the power of dialogue.[190] In short, Plato's influence reminds readers of their role as interpreters. From this perspective, one can gain a deeper understanding of the original, unifying construction of the *Klementia*, especially in comparison to the hypothetical *Grundschrift* and the *Recognitions*, positioning the *Klementinist* not merely as a compiler or redactor but rather as an author of Christian philosophical fiction who exhibits a keen interest in the hermeneutical strategies of textual interpretation.

Similar and unique reflections on proper hermeneutics in the *Klementia*, I argue, are also connected to the way in which this Christian prose emphasizes the value of storytelling and the act of reading fiction. This also entails meta-reflections on storytelling, emphasizing that the good Christian is a discerning reader who applies proper interpretative hermeneutics. Where instances of interaction with Greek novelistic prose, particularly Chariton and Achilles Tatius, are observed, there are also significant reflections on the acts of truth-telling, deception, and storytelling. These instances, absent from other *Pseudo-Clementine* versions, highlight the originality of the *Klementinist*, as I will discuss in detail.

The *Klementia* provides ample markers of fictionality that would have guided the ancient reader towards the realm of the make-believe.[191] This concept refers to a set of hermeneutical tools and techniques within the text, as well as reader-response dynamics that establish nuanced and complex relationships with truth, similar to those found in the Greek novels. These narratives simultaneously encourage belief in the world as created and

---

[189] Cf. the Myth of Thamus and Teuth; Plato, *Phaedrus* 274b–278b.
[190] De Vos, "Plato's Phaedrus and Symposium in the Pseudo-Clementine Homilies," 134–146.
[191] On this concept, see Morgan, "Make Believe," 175–229.

signal, in a sophisticated manner, the artifice and artificiality of this same world. The same occurs within the *Klementia* by means of hypertextual cases, which trigger the make-believe aspect of a fictional narrative; moreover, this Christian narrative reflects on aesthetics, morality, and cultural identity, particularly along the fault lines of the strategies surrounding this make-believe. The readers are also invited to interpret the *Klementia* and its interactions with the novelistic tradition at this hermeneutical level, where they are further challenged in their capacity as Greek *paideutic* readers. The concept of ἑλληνίζειν [*hellènizein*] plays a crucial role here, linking cultural identity as *pepaideumenos* and the *Klementia* as prose fiction.

The Process of Ἀφελληνισθῆναι *(Aphellēnisthēnai)*

A notable example of this phenomenon occurs in the scene in which Mattidia is recognized near a temple in Aradus (*Klem.* 12.12.1ff). This is part of the second half of the narrative, subsequent to Clement's baptism in *Klem.* 11. The focus shifts towards the reunion of Clement's lost family and, on Peter's request, Clement recalls how he lost his mother, brothers, and father, citing an array of unfortunate circumstances (*Klem.* 12.8–10). This sets up the sequence of recognition scenes involving Clement and his family, the first of which is the recognition of his mother in Aradus.

As has been noted by several scholars, this scene draws comparisons to Greek novelistic prose. Hansen suggests that the scene in which Clement fails to recognize his own mother (at this point a beggar, 12.22.3) resembles a scene from Heliodorus' *Aethiopica* (7.7–8), in which Theagenes fails to recognize Chariclea dressed as a beggar.[192] The problem here is one of timing, as the *Klementia* most likely predates the *Aethiopica*. In any case, as I call it, an interesting shared novelistic topic can be observed within the two narratives, which could go back to the literary motif of Odysseus dressed as beggar. Scholars like Marie-Ange Calvet-Sébasti and Paolo Liverani have instead suggested more plausible and direct parallels with Chariton's *Chaereas and Callirhoe*, noting similarities such as the thirty-stadia distance from the island to the mainland – which is factually incorrect (*Klem.* 12.12.1; *Chariton* 7.5.1; cf. *Rec.* VII.12).[193] Both scenes also feature a temple, though the one in the *Klementia* is unspecified, while Chariton specifies the temple of Aphrodite (7.5.1). These studies reveal the *Klementia*'s literary qualities and its engagement with novelistic tradition,

---

[192] Hansen, "Die Metamorphose des Heiligen Clemens," 124; cf. Kerényi, *Die griechisch-orientalische Romanliteratur*, 73–74; Montiglio, *Love and Providence*, 213.
[193] Calvet-Sébasti, "Une île romanesque," 87–99; Liverani, "Pietro Turista," 136–145.

as these attend to the shared motifs beyond the mere classification of similarities or differences. Calvet-Sébasti highlights the differing roles of Callirhoe and Mattidia in their temple scenes, in this case specifically regarding religion. While Callirhoe finds refuge, Mattidia questions religion after failing to receive divine aid.[194] Liverani and Salač here understandably assume that this potential engagement with Chariton's novel had already occurred within the *Grundschrift*,[195] as a similar scene is also incorporated in the *Recognitionist* version (*Rec.* VII.12ff). Nevertheless, as I now further discuss, the *Klementinist* deploys various strategies which address interaction with other novelistic expressions, and leverages this interaction to evoke meta-literary reflection, more than is the case in the *Recognitions* or the *Syriac* version.

This first recognition scene unfolds on the island of Aradus, where Peter's students express a desire to visit a temple, drawn by its magnificent columns and statues, accredited to the famous sculptor Phidias. However, Peter shows no interest in the aesthetic beauty of Greek art. Instead, at the temple entrance, he converses with a female beggar with deformed hands. At Peter's request, the woman recounts her tragic past, including the loss of her family and the subsequent suffering she endured (12.15–18). However, she conceals her relatives' identities, claiming her husband was Sicilian and she Ephesian (12.19.4; ἐσοφίσατο ἄλλα ἀντὶ ἄλλων εἰπεῖν καὶ ὁμῶς ἔφη αὐτὴν μὴν Ἐφεσίαν εἶναι, τὸν δὲ ἄνδρα Σικελόν). Ultimately, through Peter's probing questions, he discovers that she is, in fact, Clement's long-lost mother (12.21).

Subsequently, Peter arranges a reunion between Clement and his mother, which is followed by their journey to Laodicea, where the second recognition scene unfolds, involving the twins, Aquila and Nicetas, and their mother Mattidia (13.3–6). Peter interprets these events as signs of God's providence and as comprising part of a further shift from ἔθνος (*ethnos*) or Ἕλλην (*Hellèn*) to Christian status. Mattidia, an unbaptized pagan, is not yet authorized to dine with Clement, her baptized son; an undesirable state of affairs for a mother just reunited with her child. Mattidia wishes to be baptized immediately, having abandoned her faith in the Greek gods after offering sacrifices to the unnamed goddess of the temple in Aradus without receiving divine assistance in return (13.5). The mother pleads with Peter to baptize her and her hostess as soon as

---

[194] In both cases, Callirhoe and Mattidia are also prepared to die: the latter because of all her sorrows caused by the loss of her family (*Klem.* 12.13.5; 12.14.4–15.1; 12.18.4). Callirhoe hopes to die by the hands of the, to her unknown, Egyptian general rather than having to marry him.

[195] Liverani, "Pietro Turista," 136–145; Salač, "Die Pseudoklementinen," 45–49.

possible, so she can be reunited with her children, a request echoed by her children (13.9–11). Additionally, Mattidia claims to have remained chaste and faithful to her husband, despite experiencing significant distress from her brother-in-law's erotic advances. Peter, however, insists she is still required to fast for at least one day before baptism, as preparation for baptism must be undertaken deliberately, not merely out of a desire to be reunited with her children. Why only one day? Her sincerity, evident from her request to have her friend baptized as well, justifies, according to Peter, a one-day fast (13.11–13). The word used here is an emphatic one: ἀφελληνισθῆναι ((*aphellēnisthēnai*); *Klem.* 13.9).

In the parallel passage from the Latin *Recognitions* (VII.34), the phrase *ante instrui et doceri* is used instead, indicating that Mattidia must first be instructed by Peter in the True Prophet's teachings and come to an understanding of the true meaning of baptism. The importance of memorizing the True Prophet's teachings and following their proper (rhetorical and philosophical) sequence, or *ordo*, is key to the *Recognitions*,[196] hence the verbs *instrui* and *doceri*: Mattidia must not only engage with but also fully comprehend these teachings. This emphasis on learning is evident throughout the *Recognitions,* where concepts from rhetorical education are integrated and the intellectual training of the disciples is given explicit emphasis.[197] It is striking, for example, that in the later recognition scene involving the father and his children (VIII.1–IX.38), recognition occurs only after several days of philosophical disputations concerning the roles of man, nature, and God. The dynamics of recognition and conversion are here explicitly linked to the intellectual insights of the protagonists.

In the *Klementia*, we encounter a distinct dynamic that engages the *reader-pepaideumenos* on a higher level. For instance, in this father and children recognition scene (*Klem.* 15), emotional transformation takes precedence over philosophical debates, with Peter using the future reunion to convert Faustus soon shortly after he enters the narrative. Nevertheless, the entire scene draws on Plato's Myth of Er as a hypotext,[198] absent in the *Recognitions*. The *Klementia*'s implied reader is prompted to recognize this particular hypertextual connection and reflect on the father's deliberations on life and the afterlife. In doing so, the implied reader is called upon in his capacity as a Greek *pepaideumenos*. The same engagement is evident in Mattidia's recognition scene, marked by the emphatic verb ἀφελληνισθῆναι.

---

[196] Cf. Marti, "Ordo – ein Grundprinzip erfolgreicher Katechese," 235–240.
[197] Vielberg, "Bildung und Rhetorik in den Pseudoklementinen," 41–63.
[198] De Vos, "Living Philosophical Fiction," 53–84.

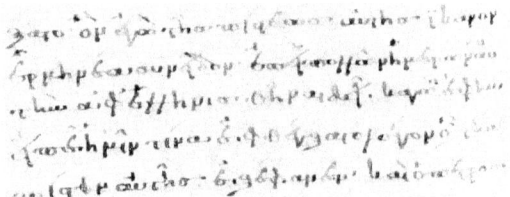

Figure 1 Codex Parisinus gr.930 *(P), folium 210v (©BnF)*

In the manuscript (O),[199] the verb ἀγνισθῆναι (*agnisthènai*) is used to present Mattidia's period of preparation for baptism as one of purification. Nevertheless, the ἀφελληνισθῆναι variant appears in the oldest manuscript P (see Figure 1), the Syriac variant (*BL Add.* 12.150),[200] and the Vormetaphrastische epitome (E) (section 106.9).

Translations and secondary literature on this passage often hesitate to translate this verb as *de-hellenize*, opting instead for interpretations like "purification" or "civilisation."[201] The prefix 'ἀπο-' suggests a process of "ceasing from," referring to non-Greeks (Romans) shedding their Greek identity, particularly in the context of polytheism. Mattidia, depicted as a beggar near Aphrodite's temple, is later recognized through divine providence but not through assistance from Greek deities like the goddess of love. This clarifies why many *Pseudo-Clementine* scholars prefer "purify" as abandoning Greek, polytheistic beliefs. The *Klementia* draws a strong distinction between Peter and his followers on the one hand and "pagans" or Ἕλληνες (*Hellènes*) on the other, a term commonly used for "pagans" from the fourth century onwards.[202] The *Klementia*, like Tatian and Tertullian, fiercely critiques Hellenism, especially its pagan religious beliefs as immoral, contagious, and sexually corrupt (e.g., *Klem.* 4.19.2–3).

---

[199] Rehm and Strecker, *Die Pseudoklementinen I*, 198.
[200] Cf. Frankenberg, *Die syrischen Clementinen*, 317.
[201] Meyboom (*De Clemens-Roman*, 262) translates this word in Dutch as "heiligen" ("to consecrate"), and in an extra footnote 262n5: "ontgriekschen" ("to strip of Greek traits"); Molland ("La circoncision," 3–6) renders it in French as "subir le catéchuménat." According to Le Boulluec et al. ("Homélies," 1473), it is best translated as "civilisée" ("civilized"), with the additional footnote (1473n9.3): "littéralement: 'pour qu'elle soit déshellénisée'" ("literally: 'so that she may be de-Hellenized'") (see also Vidalis, "Éléments, liturgiques dans le roman pseudo-clémentin" 262: "qu'elle soit civilisée"). In his German translation, Jürgen Wehnert (*Pseudoklementinische Homilien*, 197) translated the verb as "von ihrer griechischen Lebensweise befreiden" ("to emancipate [them] from their Greek mode of living"). In English scholarship, Curtis Hutt (*The Sorrows*, 97) use the translation of "purify" and, only recently, Duncan ("Eve, Mattidia, and the Gender Discourse," 181) renders the word as *de-hellenization*.
[202] Bowersock, *Hellenism*, 11.

Thus, Mattidia's *de-hellenization* is essential for transforming her religious life and beliefs.[203] Nevertheless, more is to be said about the choice of this particular word.

Rethinking Greekness

The emphatic nature of ἀφελληνισθῆναι has gone unnoticed in previous literature. It marks one's Greekness, not only in terms of religious beliefs, but also specifically regarding cultural status as a Greek *pepaideumenos*. While the connection to religious beliefs is evident, the confrontation with Greekness through the character of Mattidia also operates on other levels. This case, I argue, evokes meta-literary reflections on Greek novelistic prose and the expectations placed on the reader as *pepaideumenos*.

The word ἀφελληνισθῆναι is derived from ἑλληνίζειν (*hellènizein*), which refers to the linguistic connotation of speaking or, to a lesser extent, translating into Greek, particularly from the perspective of non-Greek speakers.[204] Classical authors usually applied the word in the neutral sense of "speaking Greek," whether as an ethnic Greek or not. In Aristotle's works, it signifies, as *terminus technicus*, the correct use of Greek language,[205] and forms, along with σαφήνεια (clarity) and πρέπον (appropiateness), the basis of proper style or λέξις (diction or speech).

After the Persian Wars, the concept of Greek identity and *hellènizein* also evolved to emphasize cultural, not just linguistic, aspects of being Greek (in contrast to "barbarian" status). Thus, even individuals of non-Greek ethnicity could become Greek in a cultural sense. This shift is evident in Isocrates' work (ca. 436–338),[206] where he considers διάνοια (thought, understanding) and παίδευσις (education) as necessary for becoming culturally *Hellèn*.

In this context, *paideia* is crucial: A culturally Greek individual is also a *pepaideumenos*. As an active and mostly intransitive verb, *hellènizein* came to indicate a process of repetitive action (*-izein/zein*) and behavior aimed at becoming Greek in both language and culture, or *paideia*.[207] Even in rare instances where attempts are made to coerce non-Greeks into Hellenization, it still reflects their active participation.[208]

---

[203] Cf. Duncan, *Novel Hermeneutics*, 135–137.
[204] Cf. Rochet, "Remarques," 175–204.
[205] *Rhet.* III.5.1407a19.
[206] Cf. Jaeger, "The Rhetoric of Isocrates," 119–141.
[207] Cf. Strohm, "'Hellenisch' als Wertbegriff," 1–13; Petersmann, "Zur Entstehung der hellenistischen Koine," 322; Rochet, "Remarques," 183–184.
[208] Wallace-Hadrill, *Rome's Cultural Revolution*, 6.

Greek culture in the Hellenistic era was closely tied to increasing power dynamics. "Barbarians" adopting Greek culture gained greater opportunities in administration and other power structures in Hellenistic politics. In the context of the Second Sophistic, when the Greek Eastern world fell under Roman dominance, Greek cultural identity and the status of *pepaideumenos* became fundamental.[209] *Paideia* emerged as a crucial factor in political and economic power discourses, as well as outward elite status, fostering a new Greek identity in the (Eastern) Roman-dominated world.[210] Thus, the notion of *hellènizein* delves into the core of culture, *paideia*, and power in the Greco-Roman sphere. New derivatives of *hellènizein* with additional prefixes also emerged in the Imperial period.

In this particular instance in the *Klementia*, we encounter a passive form of the verb with the prefix ἀπο-. The verb itself is rarely used. Aside from the *Klementia*, only three extant, non-Christian, witnesses from the first centuries use this verb.[211] In Philo's *Legatio ad Gaium* (section 147.5), the verb (ἀφελληνίσας) refers to Augustus' hellenizing of barbaric nations, which seems an exception to the verb's usual intransitive aspect.[212] The second-century rhetorician Julius Pollux' *Onomasticon* (section 5.154.6) employs the word as an explanatory synonym for Ἑρμηνεὺς καὶ ἑρμηνευτής, one who translates into Greek. The third case is found in Favorinus of Arelate's *Thirty-seventh Oration*, or the so-called *Corinthian Oration,* in which Favorinus, a well-known member of the so-called Second Sophistic and student of Dio Chrysostomus, emphasizes three aspects of his self-identification: being a Gaul, being a Roman, and, above all, being an accomplished Greek in terms of language, education, and culture, thus *paideia*. This highlights the connection between *Bildung* as a prerequisite for culture and the formation of cultural identity in the Second Sophistic.[213]

In the *Corinthian Oration*, Favorinus urges the Corinthian inhabitants to preserve the statue erected in his honor, now that he has fallen out of favor with the emperor. His bronze statue, positioned at the library, represents a symbol of *paideia* (section 37.25–26). Favorinus even asserts that statues of him be placed in every city to serve as symbols and

---

[209] For the dynamics of Roman imperialism, Hellenization, and groups as Jews and Iranians in the Hellenistic period, see Momigliano, *Alien Wisdom*.
[210] Bowersock, *Hellenism*, 7; Borg, *Paideia*.
[211] Cf. Wallace-Hadrill (*Rome's Cultural Revolution*, 5–7) who does not mention the *Klementia*.
[212] See Delling, "Philons Enkomion," 189; Inglebert, *Histoire*, 438–440.
[213] Wallace-Hadrill, *Rome's Cultural Revolution*, 33.

transmitters of Greekness between the divine and his public (section 26).[214] Here, ἀφελληνισθῆναι signals completion of a process, with the prefix ἀπο- suggesting finality. One has made oneself fully Hellenic, or at least within one's possibilities. The concept of *hellēnizein* was particularly prominent in the Second Sophistic, as individuals increasingly focused on Greek culture and heritage amid increasing Roman dominance.[215] This preoccupation with *Greekness* is also explored by Favorinus, who examines what exactly it means to be Greek culturally and linguistically as a Roman (member of the *ordo equester*), just as the Corinthians have learned to live as Greeks while originally being a colony of Roman citizens.[216]

Becoming a *paideumenos*, as a non-Greek in a Roman-dominated world, is a painstaking process.[217] In his *Oration* (section 26), Favorinus seeks to remind the Corinthians of their city's history, from its sacking in 146 BC to its refounding as a Roman city by Julius Caesar in 44 BC. By presenting himself as an accomplished Greek *pepaideumenos*, Favorinus resonates with the Corinthians, who, as Romans, have also adopted a Greek cultural identity. This context serves as the "perfect backdrop for Favorinus' mimetic self-making,"[218] positioning Hellenism as a cultural and intellectual framework for evaluating Romans, a perspective similarly reflected in Plutarch's *Parallel Lives*.[219] Only by recognizing Favorinus as the accomplished Greek *pepaideumenos*, albeit self-proclaimed, can the Corinthians truly become Greek.

This raises fundamental questions about the spectrum of Greek identity, particularly for non-Greeks, and its connection to *paideia*. These themes of *paideia*, cultural identity, and Greekness, as observed in the Second Sophistic, also appear in Greek prose fiction. In erotic novels such as those of Chariton and Heliodorus, issues concerning what it means to behave or be recognized as a "Greek" are present (e.g., Chariton 4.8.2; Heliodorus 2.12.4; 2.30.1; 7.14.2; 10.9.6; 10.31.1). Greekness is approached as part of a larger cultural process in which the reader participates. The question of what precisely constitutes Greek identity remains one of the most debated topics in past scholarship on the Greek erotic novels.[220] For example, Whitmarsh discusses how centripetal forces, as in returning to the Greek

---

[214] Cf. König, "Favorinus'," 141–171; Brod, "The Upright Man," 136–137.
[215] Cf. Bowie, "Hellenes," 183–204.
[216] Wallace-Hadrill, *Rome's Cultural Revolution*, 5.
[217] Whitmarsh, "Greece," 304.
[218] Whitmarsh, *Greek Literature*, 121, 128–129.
[219] Whitmarsh, *Greek Literature*, 117.
[220] Cf. Whitmarsh, *Narrative and Identity in the Ancient Greek Novel*, particularly part II "Narrative and Identity."

homeland, and centrifugal forces, as in the spirit of adventure, influence the construction of Greek identity. He argues that novelistic prose:

> ... embodies a particular way of expressing the relationship between self and society, one that could be identified over a long period as characteristically Greek, while also accommodating the radical changes that Greek identity underwent over four centuries.[221]

Whitmarsh argues that erotic prose "seems to express not a generalized Greek cultural identity but a very specific variant of it, predicated on a sense of 'decenteredness'."[222] For example, in Heliodorus' novel, the protagonist, an extremely beautiful "Greek" girl, is revealed to be the white daughter of the Ethiopian royal family, highlighting the dynamic aspects of Greek identity in the Eastern Roman Empire. Other Greek erotic prose works, such as those of Chariton, Xenophon, and Achilles Tatius, alongside the broader Second Sophistic environment, also constitute part of this broader literary and aesthetic history, reflecting on the self within the Greek world and the spectrum of "Greekness," from well-trained cultural Greek to cultural "barbarian."[223]

I argue that these dynamics of Greek identity formation permeate the essence of Greek novelistic prose and also penetrate to the Greek *Klementia*'s core. In the third and fourth centuries, debates between Christian and non-Christian intellectuals, who often shared a common educational background as *pepaideumenoi*, centered on what it means to be "Greek." Gregory of Nazianzus, in his invectives against Julian, explores the religious and linguistic connotations of *hellēnizein*.[224] In his fourth *Oration* (section 107–108), he pointedly questions Julian as to whether Hellenism is "your monopoly." The *Klementinist*, aware of similar debates, engages with novelistic tradition as part of original Christian fiction to demonstrate his aesthetic and moral reflections on Greekness, deriving from the very "genre" of erotic prose itself. The reader is expected to engage with this framework hermeneutically, however, unlike the implicit reader of Greek erotic novels;[225] the *Klementia*'s reader must also employ hermeneutical strategies to correctly interpret Gospel traditions and Old Testament narratives.

---

[221] Whitmarsh, *Narrative and Identity in the Ancient Greek Novel*, 139.
[222] Whitmarsh, *Narrative and Identity in the Ancient Greek Novel*, 255.
[223] See also Goldhill, *Being Greek*.
[224] Gregorius Nazianzus, "Oratio IV – Contra Julianum I," 35.633c–649b.
[225] For a discussion of the Greek novels' readership, see, e.g., Bowie ("The Ancient Readers," 87–106), who defends the theory of a learned readership (which I also support); according to Perry (*The Ancient Romances*, 5), the audience was "poor in spirit."

Meta-Literary Tensions Regarding Ἀφελληνισθῆναι (Aphellēnisthênai): How (Not) to Read as a Greek

Thus, ἀφελληνισθῆναι is a highly dynamic term that goes beyond its purely "religious" connotation, encompassing cultural, aesthetic, and moral dimensions of Greek identity. This is particularly significant in the context of Mattidia's *de-hellenization*, a process explicitly referenced by the term ἀφελληνισθῆναι. Notably, this process is depicted as painful, as Mattidia seeks *de-hellenization* in her role as a Roman. This transformation extends beyond the religious sphere to intellectual and cultural domains. The presence of ἀφελληνισθῆναι in the symbolically rich scene of Mattidia's recognition challenges the reader to reflect on the dynamics of Greek *pepaideumenos* identity and, furthermore, the nature of Greek novelistic prose, which goes beyond mere *delectare* (to entertain).

Mattidia's recognition scene engages closely with other expressions of Greek novelistic erotic prose. Mattidia exemplifies values of *sophrosunè* (temperance) and marital fidelity that are equally important in Greek novelistic prose, such as Chariton's heroine Callirhoe, and other Greek literature. The reader is expected to approach Mattidia as a Greek heroine, who is, however, positioned as Callirhoe's antithesis, notably in terms of the aforementioned opposition between Greek identity and *theosebès* (God-worshipper). In Chariton's novel, the goddess of the temple, Aphrodite, drives the recognition scene,[226] while this same goddess is powerless to intercede in the *Klementia*. Instead, divine providence and Peter serve as the primary driving forces behind the recognitions. As Edwards notes, the Christian response introduces a meta-narrative element: neither Aphrodite, Eros, nor Tychè hold true power, prompting reflection on desire and divine power.[227]

The antithetical relationship between the two heroines raises meta-discursive tension, encouraging the reader to consider not only divine intervention, but also the literary discourse concerning the portrayal of "beauty" in relation to the true heroine (and hero) in Greek novelistic prose.

Seduced to Reading Beauty

In the *Klementia, beauty* is subjected to a strict interpretive framework: physical beauty, even if allegedly divine, is not to be gazed upon, except for God's beauty as described in *Klem.* 17.9–10. In the seventeenth book, Peter

---

[226] Cf. Montiglio, *Love and Providence*, 220–221.
[227] Edwards, "The *Clementina*," 466–469; see also Côté, "Les *Pseudo-Clémentines* et le choix du roman grec," 480.

counters one of Simon's critiques. Simon claims that while Peter rejects the physical forms of divine statues as comprising part of false polytheistic belief, he paradoxically proposes another, more unsettling idea: that God possesses a human form. With an original theory, Peter responds that God's form is purely noetic, to be contemplated as the true Beauty. This introduces a philosophical, even Neoplatonic concept, in which one experiences Beauty through intellectual contemplation. This intellectual engagement links the soul's yearning pursuit for God as the ultimate embodiment of Beauty:[228]

> ... and if they be separated from the body and be found with a longing for Him (πόθον ἔχουσαι), they are borne along into His bosom, as in the winter time the mists of the mountains, attracted by the rays of the sun, are borne along immortal to it. What affection (στοργὴν) ought therefore to arise within us if we gaze with our mind on His beautiful shape (ἐὰν τὴν εὐμορφίαν αὐτοῦ τῷ νῷ κατοπτεύσωμεν)! But otherwise it is absurd to speak of beauty. For beauty cannot exist apart from shape (ἀδύνατον γὰρ **κάλλος** ἄνευ μορφῆς εἶναι); nor can one be attracted to the love of God, nor even deem that he can see Him, if God has no form (καὶ πρὸς τὸν αὐτοῦ **ἔρωτα** ἐπισπᾶσθαί τινα ἢ καὶ δοκεῖν θεὸν ὁρᾶν εἶδος οὐκ ἔχοντα).[229]

The first recognition scene of the *Klementia* can be understood within the broader literary and philosophical context of noetic contemplation of Beauty (in *Klem.* 17), which is original in comparison to other *Pseudo-Clementine* traditions. Peter's students express a desire to visit the Greek temple with its statues crafted by the renowned Phidias. However, Peter deliberately turns away from this "Greek" spectacle, focusing instead on a disfigured beggar. This contrasts with the lavish references to Callirhoe's beauty (6.7–10) in the similar temple setting in Chariton's novel, where she resides in the Royal Chamber of the Persian Queen during the Egypt–Persia war, her beauty having raised her even to celebrity status.

It is a well-known topos to introduce novelistic protagonists through allusion to their extraordinary physical beauty. For instance, Chariton's Chaereas surpasses Achilles and Alcibiades in beauty (1.1), while the eponymous hero from Longus' *Daphnis and Chloe* is introduced as a beautiful baby (1.2). Similarly, Apollonius' beauty is emphasized early on in Philostratus' *Life of Apollonius of Tyana* (1.7.1; 1.8), while Xenophon's Habrocomes grows more handsome daily (1.1). Even Heliodorus' wounded hero, Theagenes, radiates "manly beauty" (*Aethiopica* 1.2).[230] Female

---

[228] Cf. De Vos, "From the Dark Platonic Cave," 253–256.
[229] Roberts and Donaldson, *Ante-Nicene Christian Library Vol. XVII*, 264–265; Rehm and Strecker, *Pseudoklementinen I*, 235.
[230] Cf. Schmeling, "Callirhoe," 37.

heroines, too, are introduced through beauty, with Callirhoe representing the quintessential example of a novelistic, celebrated allure. This strategy of beauty, and also of *eugeneia* (nobility of birth), of the heroine is also adopted in pre- and post-Constantinian *Passiones*, reflecting the literary influence of Greek novels.[231]

Callirhoe's stream of beauty, symbolized in her name, serves as a central narrative force, attracting suitors and crowds wherever she goes (1.1.16; 2.3.9; 3.2.15–17 in Milete; 3.2.17; 5.3.9–10 in Babylon). She is compared to a queen bee, drawing swarms of people (2.3.10), even entire populations of cities (5.5.8). Callirhoe is frequently likened to divinities, especially Aphrodite, when she resides at the temple of the goddess, and the link between Callirhoe and the statue of Aphrodite is often referenced (2.3.6). Callirhoe's beauty is not just physical but is also symbolic of inner divinity.[232] Her appearance aboard the ship bound for her wedding in Miletus can even be interpreted as an epiphany of Aphrodite (3.2.14). Her beauty is also linked to her *eugeneia* or noble birth, as, despite finding herself sold into slavery, her beauty continues to radiate nonetheless (1.10.6; 2.2.1–3; 2.5.6).

Callirhoe's beauty not only attracts crowds but also drives her story and the adventures that unfold within, bringing her both joy and misfortune.[233] In 6.6.4, Callirhoe reflects on how her beauty has caused many of her misfortunes. Her beauty triggers her marriage to Chaereas, whose jealousy over her beauty leads to their separation and even her apparent death. However, her beauty also facilitates her recognition with her lost husband on the island of Aradus. This motif, where a heroine's beauty leads to suffering and, on a meta-literary level, enduring stories and novels recounting it, is a well-known motif within Greek literature, mirroring the myth of the most beautiful of all women and celebrity par excellence among the Greeks: Helen of Troy. Helen's beauty, for instance, seizes the attention of all the embattled Greek and Trojan warriors when she appears atop the Trojan walls (*Il.* 3.86–94), leaving the Trojan king Priam and his retinue, including the elders and all other spectators, in astonishment. Who could blame the Trojans and Greeks for fighting over her (*Il.* 3.141–160)? It is therefore no coincidence that Chariton compares Callirhoe to Helen throughout the novel. For example, Dionysius, Callirhoe's second husband from Asia Minor, fears men will abduct her just as Paris did with Helen (5.2.8). Furthermore, Callirhoe herself expresses concern

---

[231] Cf. Cataudella, "Vite di Santo e romanzo," 934.
[232] Cf. Zeitlin, "Living Portraits," 38; Schmeling, "Callirhoe," 46.
[233] Cf. Haynes, *Fashioning the Feminine in the Greek Novel*, 47.

over future poets recounting her misfortunes (5.5.3), evoking the same anxieties as experienced by Helen herself (*Il.* 6.357–358), who wonders in a conversation with Hector whether her relationship with Paris and her other misfortunes were part of a divine scheme meant to be immortalized by future poets. Thus, beauty, divinity, and storytelling have been intricately intertwined since the dawn of Greek literature. This connection is still evident in Callirhoe, and the Greek readers are reminded of it through their act of reading.

The focus here extends beyond the beauty of the heroines merely serving as narrative catalysts, also encompassing how beauty is described and experienced, particularly by crowds and suitors. The reader-*pepaideumenos* is provided with an expected framework of rhetorical descriptions and erotic *ekphraseis* (a rhetorical device indicating the vividness of written descriptions of a particular person or work of art). Callirhoe, characterized as a "demagogue" (δημαγωγός; 4.1.10), draws attention through her physical beauty,[234] with the narrative reinforcing this attraction with erotic *ekphraseis* and references to other renowned Greek heroines and divinities, enticing the reader to enjoy and engage with its literary effects.

Beauty, on a meta-literary level, therefore drives narratives and *histories* and attracts readers through rhetorical descriptions of beauty and the misfortunes it causes. The *Klementinist* scene featuring Mattidia introduces a distinct discourse, however. Although the family's history of misfortune begins with the brother-in-law's attempt to seduce Mattidia, her beauty is not a focal point in the narrative; rather, the lack of it stands out. The opening of the *Pseudo-Clementine* literature presents an anti-hero. Clement is sick, distressed, and literally turning pale due to his assumed ignorance of the truth. Here, we do not encounter a hero characterized by radiating beauty. Rather, we face a more rigid meta-discursive project. Mattidia is not depicted as a heroine admired for her beauty in Aradus, she makes for no celebrity, and her lack of beauty is explicitly contrasted with the beauty of Phidias' statues, admired by Peter's students. While Callirhoe is often implicitly compared to Helen of Troy, this same Helen assumes a counter-role within the *Klementia*, as the ultimate example of deceptive beauty and immoral adultery, instigating the devastating war between Greeks and "barbarians" (*Klem.* 2.23).

Moreover, Mattidia's loss of beauty is not merely a superficial disguise, but a profound transformation, distinguishing her from typical portrayals of novelistic heroines and also from other, Christian hagiographic heroines,

---

[234] Cf. Schmeling, "Callirhoe," 46–47.

including the transvestite saints, who themselves are also a reaction to the Greek novelistic heroine-discourses.[235] For instance, a harlot-saint like Pelagia,[236] or a heroine like Thecla from the *Acts of Paul and Thecla*, deliberately denounce their feminine beauty and any trace of potentially perceived attractiveness in a reaction against worldly desires and pernicious flesh. While Mattidia does indeed lose her beauty, she regains it through her connection with Peter, ultimately restoring her role as wife and mother. In the *Klementia*, both marriage and sexuality are viewed positively (e.g., 2.15.1). Mattidia thus serves as an intermediate figure between novelistic and Christian heroines of the *Apocryphal Acts* and hagiographical literature, reflecting the concept of *sophrosunè* (temperance).[237] In the novels, protagonists are often depicted as *sophron*, maintaining chastity throughout various adventures, ultimately restoring disrupted marriages and emphasizing the importance of sex within marriage. Leucippe describes enduring tortures to remain chaste for Cleitophon (Ach. Tat. 5.18.4), and Callirhoe refuses to marry a leader of the opposite army (later revealed as her husband Chaereas; Char. 7.6.8). In Heliodorus' novel, Chariclea even states that no force whatsoever could make her surrender her virginity to anyone but Theagenes (1.25.4).

In novelistic discourse, however, these themes are often described ambiguously, intertwining irony, violence, desire, and transgression of boundaries, and undermining the protagonist's allegedly ideal, chaste nature.[238] Readers themselves are also seduced by descriptions of physical beauty and sexual encounters, challenging their own chastity. In contrast, heroines in the *Apocryphal Acts*, such as Thecla, heroines of martyr acts and transvestite saints, firmly reject physical beauty, marriage,[239] and sexual consummation, making *sophrosunè* a sexless virtue. Mattidia, however, represents a more restrained but sex-positive narrative. She safeguards her *sophrosunè* from her brother-in-law and the lascivious

---

[235] In the *Apocryphal Acts*, interactions with novelistic tradition are used to demonstrate the quasi-romantic attachment between the chaste heroine and the apostle. This is part of a complex and subversive strategy that surpasses the *coattail theory*: it involves an inversion of the strategies of Eros and the disruption of sexual relations between novelistic heroines and heroes; cf. Hägg, *The Novel*, 154–165; Cooper, *The Virgin*, 45–67.

[236] Cf. Van Pelt, *Saints in Disguise*.

[237] Cf. North, *Sophrosyne*, for a general discussion of this concept.

[238] See Goldhill, *Foucault's Virginity*.

[239] There are some heroines of martyr acts who first aspire to marry, but are convinced by Christian preachers to abandon marriage (such as Domitilla in the *Passio Nerei et Achillei*), while others, like Caecilia in the *Passio Caeciliae*, marry but convince their partners to embrace a spiritual marriage (cf. Bossu et al., "The Saint as Cunning Heroine," 433–452).

gazes of other men, including the author's, who refrains from describing her beauty in seductive fashion. This absence of specific (and erotic) detail tempers the expectations of the Greek *pepaideumenoi*, contrasting sharply with the stories of Callirhoe and Helen, who are frequently subject to alluring description.[240] Although Mattidia shares fundamental values with Greek novelistic heroines, such as *sophrosunè,* her characterization extends these notions more profoundly and challenges novelistic conventions. On a meta-discursive level, Mattidia is *de-hellenized* by not being subjected to erotic gaze typical of the Greco-Roman novel.

This theme contributes to a broader meta-narrative discourse within the *Klementia* regarding true Beauty – i.e., God's form – but also regarding the performance of reading novelistic prose and the reader's desire for salacious details. Notably, the actual adventures of the family members are minimally detailed. For instance, the brother-in-law's actions and Mattidia's future suitors remain largely unexplored.[241] Instead, the adventures and misfortunes catalyzed by Mattidia's beauty are presented only as part of brief testimonies during the recognition scenes. By this point, the family members have already been scattered around the world, and it is the account of Peter and his disciples that drive the reader along the Mediterranean voyage. In this respect, we encounter what I call meta-novelistic prose: rather than focusing on interventions of Eros or ambiguous stories that beauty incites, the reader is offered Peter's interpretations, framing the family's history as guided by God's providence, of whom alone the beauty is described in the *Klementia* (*Klem.* 17) in philosophical terms.

Moreover, another aspect of meta-narrative discourse, Mattidia exhibits a deeper form of *paideia* in her efforts to steer the course of her own story, which unfolds as a chaste (*sophron*) narrative in which she emerges as her own heroine. This represents an original core aspect of the *Klementia*, fundamentally linked to broader engagement with interpretation and storytelling. Here the reader, within the dynamics regarding *aphellènisthènai*, is rather confronted with reflections on how to interpret the chaste *historia* surrounding Clement's family, rather than simply *delectare* in the many *ekphraseis*.

---

[240] Cf. Nilsson, "Desire and God Have Always Been Around," 235–260, for the erotic discourse in the ancient novel, Christian writings – Apocryphal Acts, vitae, passions – and Byzantine novels.

[241] Only in a later tradition of the Latin *Pseudo-Clementines*, namely in a Croatian eighteenth-century manuscript of the *Gesta Sancti Clementis*, more details are offered, among which the name of the brother-in-law, Flavius; cf. Cerno, *Un frammento inedito.*

A Curious Apostle and Deceptive Stories

Although the recognition scenes are framed as the result of divine providence, there is something else noteworthy at play. The immediate catalyst of the recognition scenes is curiosity, *periergia* (περιεργία) or *polypragmosunè* (πολυπραγμοσύνη), particularly in relation to misfortune and storytelling. For instance, Clement's father enters the narrative after secretly observing Peter and his group from a distance at the seashore. He is driven by curiosity (περιέργῳ) regarding their affairs, their reasons for prayer, and the nature of their beliefs. His own life experiences, as he recounts them, are not perceived as shaped by divine providence but by astrological determinism (*Klem.* 14.2.2–3). The *Klementinist* establishes a strong connection between curiosity and the hermeneutics of story, or, in this case, Faust's own life story. This curiosity is mirrored by Peter himself, who becomes intrigued by the physical mutilation of Mattidia sitting at the temple entrance, rather than being drawn by some beautiful appearance (*Klem.* 12.14.3–4). Peter's interest is directed towards other people's affairs, including their stories and misfortunes:

> What is it that grieves you? I should like to know, O woman. For if you inform me, in return for this favor, I shall satisfy you that souls live in Hades; and instead of precipice or pool, I shall give you a drug (φάρμακον), that you may live and die without torment.[242]

A striking term in this context is *φάρμακον*, which again strengthens the link between storytelling and narrative interpretation. Danny Praet elucidated in his analysis of this passage that the connection between storytelling and the concept of *φάρμακον* (*pharmakon*) dates back to Homer and Plato:

> The sophistication in this passage is that Peter is referring in a very novelistic context to the truth, to a true story, which will lead Mattidia to the Truth, but Peter uses a word which conjures up a whole tradition of invented stories from the *Odyssey* over Plato to this Christian novel about the True Prophecy. Mattidia is comparable to Helen because she left her husband but from the crucial moral point of view, she is the exact opposite of Helen: where the latter was the most famous adulteress of Antiquity eloping from Greece with her Trojan lover, Mattidia left for Greece to get away from an adulterous lover in Rome, mythologically linked to Troy. In Homer, Helen adds a real "pharmakon" to the wine of her guests before she starts to tell her own story in book 4 of the Odyssey. Peter will give Mattidia her "pharmakon" by telling her what really happened to her family.[243]

---

[242] Roberts and Donaldson, *Ante-Nicene Christian Library Vol. XVII*, 199; Rehm and Strecker, *Pseudoklementinen I*, 181.

[243] Praet, "Truth-telling, Lying and False Wisdom in the *Pseudo-Clementine*," 195.

The focus here is not only on the appropriate hermeneutics of storytelling, but, as I argue, also on curiosity about the stories themselves, particularly how individuals experience their own life stories. This mirrors a pattern familiar to Greek readers, especially those acquainted with Greek novels. As Richard Hunter observes, "both the novelist and his readers, concerned to discover 'what is going on', are *curiosi*."[244] Readers of the novel are often confronted with their own curiosity, driven by an interest in others' affairs and misfortunes. This preoccupation is, of course, key to novelistic discourse: interest and entertainment derives from the series of unfortunate events that befall family members and lovers. Chariton, at the outset of his final book, explicitly acknowledges, and even manipulates, this dynamic,[245] stating his final book is the "sweetest" as it describes the upright love and lawful marriage of the couple, serving as a "recompense for the grim events of the earlier books" (καθάρσιον γάρ ἐστι τῶν ἐν τοῖς πρώτοις σκυθρωπῶν; 8.1.4)".[246] This shift counters the potential excess of *polypragmosunè* on the part of the reader, who was drawn into much engagement with the misfortunes (κακά) of others as told in the previous books.

Of course, precisely such engagement with calamity and grim misfortune arouses the reader's curiosity.[247] In his essay on this topic, Plutarch describes how curiosity is inseparable from interest in stories (*historiai*, *plasmata*) of misfortune, jealousy, and the toppling of kingdoms (517e–f). Roman Emperor Julian's *Epistle 89* (301b) may even criticize such stories for lacking historical basis, a passage often interpreted as a reference to erotic novels, though this remains debated.[248] Whether or not Julian specifically refutes Greek erotic prose, Plutarch highlights the reader's curiosity about histories (ἱστορίας) involving seduction of virgins, adultery, and misfortunes (κακά; 517e–f), rather than being drawn to positive news (518a), eliciting sleep inducing boredom. Precisely this readerly inclination is deliberately engaged with by the *Klementia*, as Peter inquires about the misfortunes of

---

[244] Hunter, "The Curious Incident," 51.
[245] Whitmarsh, "The Greek Novel," 606.
[246] Chariton, *Callirhoe*, 360–361.
[247] *Polypragmosunè* as curiosity for stories is a longstanding literary and philosophical motif in Greek literature, including in Plato. In the *Symposium*'s opening chapter, Apollodorus exhibits insatiable curiosity about Socrates' life. These feelings of curiosity will also influence later philosophical novels. In works like Lucian's *Onos* and Apuleius' *Metamorphoses*, the inquisitive heroes' insatiable curiosity lead to their own misfortune. It is a distortion of the philosophic desire for wisdom (cf. Hunter, "Plato's *Symposium*," 295–312), but it is in their mischievous behavior that the reader finds delight.
[248] Hunter, "The Curious Incident," 57; *Contra* Whitmarsh, "The Greek Novel," 607–608.

the disabled beggar, not a beautiful Helen-like protagonist: he desires to hear her story, thus also encouraging the reader's desire for narrative closure.

An interesting passage in this respect can be observed in Petronius' *Satyricon*, a novel renowned for its curiosities, bizarre spectacles, and extravagant dishes that, while remarkable, are in fact deceptive to their nature, whereby one desires to enjoy but also to expose the illusion. Within this context, Encolpius' curiosity compels him to inquire about a woman moving through the dining room, later revealed to be Fortunata, the wife of the host and *libertus* Trimalchio (*Sat.* 37.1). Such an interest in the affairs of a woman is also discussed at length in Plutarch's essay, likening it to adultery (519b; 522a) as "an undressing of other men's secrets."[249] Similarly, Peter's curiosity about the handicapped beggar's story shifts the reader's focus towards an interest in the identity and troubles of a female character who makes an entrance within a setting that has an important novelistic counterpart.

Notably, Peter's curiosity about such misfortunes seems distant, as he derives little enjoyment from these testimonies and stories, which lack vivid descriptions of suffering. This moment signals a shift in novelistic discourse, in which curiosity in stories plays a role, however devoid of erotic ambiguity and (dis)tastefully salacious details. Of particular importance here is not only that we observe a distinction from Greek prose fiction regarding the topos of curiosity in relation to the narrative characters and the implied reader, but that this discourse also contrasts with various *Apocryphal Acts* and the way in which the protagonist-apostles and the subjects of their curiosity are characterized. For example, in the fourth-century *Apocryphal Acts of Andrew and Mathew* (AAMt), as Jason König rightly observes, apostles intentionally avoid engagement with spectacular, even grotesque, events that would typically captivate a Greek audience, yet the narrative includes exuberant details of even horrifying scenes, like the Myrmidonians' blood-extracting machine (section 22) and their cannibalistic quench for blood (section 23), engaging the reader with the voyeuristic, sensationalistic conventions of Greco-Roman novel writing.[250]

This point relates to a pattern of expectations aimed at the Greek reader. In fiction, cannibalism often symbolizes, on a meta-literary level, textual consumption and the parasitic relationship between text and reader.[251] In the *AAMt*, Christian discourse adopts this register of the grotesque, as illustrated in the account of how Andrew prays for a wall of fire around a

---

[249] Hunter, "The Curious Incident," 54.
[250] König, "Novelistic and Anti-Novelistic Narrative," 121–149.
[251] Kilgour, *From Communion to Cannibalism*; regarding Petronius: Rimell, *Petronius*.

city to confine the cannibalistic inhabitants within, and bitter water rising to consume them, leading to their repentance and conversion (section 29). The motif of the grotesque is hence literally incorporated into a Christian discourse and the motif of grotesque cannibalism becomes a spiritual symbol, as observed in section 28, where the blood of Andrew, being dragged through the streets, produces fruit-bearing trees, enabling the faithful to partake in the apostle's flesh (see also section 32). Thus, cannibalism and the grotesque are reimagined, even devoured, as Christian spiritual motifs in the fourth-century *Acts*, contrasting with the gory, physical descriptions of the non-Christians. The Christian discourse engages the reader's predilection for grotesque and cannibalistic imagery, yet subverts them on a meta-discursive level. It is through this hermeneutic interpretation that the reader is confronted with how the physical, gory, and grotesque events in question are literally ignored by Andrew, who displays no interest whatever in foreign and non-Christian culture,[252] yet these events are described (by the narrating voice) in detail for the supposed Greek reader, aiming to facilitate confrontation with the spiritual reinterpretation of themes of cannibalism and the grotesque by means of the apostle's focalization. As König concludes, readers must choose between a novelistic, "ethnographic thrill we potentially feel as readers," and the anti-novelistic, "utterly incurious gaze of the apostles."[253]

In the early-fourth-century *Klementia*, grotesque descriptions are hinted at but not fully explored. The ambiguous tension present in the *AAMt* is partially retained in the *Klementia*, as Peter permits his disciples to behold the splendor of Phidias' statues, while readers are denied access to this spectacle – or, more precisely, to read about it. This is also evident in other scenes. At the end of the narrative, a curious face-swap scene occurs between Simon and Clement's father, Faustus, allowing Simon to flee undetected to Antioch. In Antioch, he spreads rumors about Peter being a magician and murderer, whereupon the Greek Antiochenes feel the desire (γλίχομαι, a rare verb) to taste Peter's very flesh. These cannibalistic tendencies align with the giants in *Klem.* 8. According to Peter's Enochian-inspired interpretation of *Gen.* 6:1–4, sexual intercourse between angels and human women led to the birth of violent and fearsome giants, who experienced an unquenchable hunger for flesh (*Klem.* 8.15.4). However, the reader receives no further

---

[252] In sections 4–5, Andrew does not exhibit any curiosity in non-Christian persons; in section 8, a flute-girl intensely looks at Andrew, who simply does not respond. He has no interest whatsoever in the strange, erotic, non-Christian culture, which for König ("Novelistic and Anti-Novelistic Narrative," 139) is a sign of the "confidence of Christian identity."

[253] König, "Novelistic and Anti-Novelistic Narrative," 142 and 140.

details on the cannibalistic thirst of the giants – who ultimately drown in a flood sent by God and whose demonic souls survive to be rebranded as Greek gods – nor of the cannibalistic audience in Antioch. Peter, like a true strategist, turns Simon's ruse to his own advantage by sending Faustus – still wearing Simon's face – to Antioch to proclaim Peter's integrity and to denounce Simon as notorious deceiver. Unlike Andrew, who overcomes the Myrmidonians' cannibalistic inclinations through grotesque miracles, Peter avoids such displays. Instead, by means of a combination of open confession and deceptive stories, he redirects public hostility towards the figure of "Simon." Peter's approach proves effective, as a messenger soon reports that Faustus, as Simon, now fears for his own life. Peter responds rather laconically, delaying his departure for Antioch by three days to appoint a bishop over Laodicea, which marks the conclusion of the *Klementinist* narrative. On a meta-literary and hermeneutic level, this scene contrasts with the *AAMt*'s indulgence in grotesque elements. Readers are limited to Peter's narrated ruse rather than indulging as *curiosus* in the grotesque scenes of a cannibalistic audience attempting to devour the apostle-protagonist(s). The *Klementia* thus not only showcases an alternative take on a novelistic topos, but also presents a different Christian meta-literary choice compared to the fourth-century *AAMt* and its "parasitic" adaptation of novelistic discourse. The grotesque is merely alluded to in the *Klementia*, leaving the Greek reader's curiosity for the grotesque unfulfilled.

Nevertheless, in the *Klementia*, the apostle displays curiosity, unlike other apostolic protagonists of apocryphal narratives. However, his curiosity pertains only to stories, aligning with conventional Greco-Roman interest in misfortune and love affairs. Yet, unlike the voyeuristic, sensationalist conventions of Greco-Roman prose, which even permeate into the *AAMt*, the *Klementia* avoids lurid descriptions of suffering and erotic advances. For instance, no detailed descriptions of Mattidia's misfortune are given. Instead, the reader's focus, as part of the larger dynamic of *aphellènisthènai*, shifts to the hermeneutical task of interpreting the various testimonies recounted in the adventures. However, the novelistic topoi of separation, adventures, pirates, and shipwrecks appear only as brief flashbacks shared by the characters. Precisely these stories and their hermeneutics function as tokens of recognition between the estranged family members,[254] rather than Mattidia's physical appearance, unlike, for

---

[254] This represents one reason why scholars consider a possible direct link with the *Historia Apollonii regis Tyri*, in which the witnesses are also tokens for recognition of other family members (cf. Montiglio, *Love and Providence*, 213–214).

example, Callirhoe, whose beauty alone serves as the token of recognition (Chariton 8.1.7). Based on Clement's earlier testimonies (*Klem.* 12.8–10; par. *Rec.* 7.8–10), the reader is familiar with the basic story outline and is subsequently offered multiple perspectives on what happened: Mattidia's account (*Klem.* 12.15–18; par. *Rec.* VII.16–18), Peter's suspicions after hearing Mattidia's testimony (*Klem.* 12.20; par. *Rec.* VII.20), Peter's retelling of Mattidia's story to Nicetas and Aquila (*Klem.* 13.2; para. *Rec.* VII.26.1), the twins' recognition of Mattidia as their mother, in Laodicea (*Klem.* 13.6–8; par. *Rec.* VII.32–33), and finally, the account of the lost husband in Laodicea (*Klem.* 14.6–7, par. *Rec.* IX.32–33).

A Metafictional Heroine and the Invention of Moral, *De-hellenized* Stories

Peter's interest in stories leads him to encounter those that are deceptive. Mattidia's testimony is partly fabricated, as she pretends to be Ephesian and claims her husband is Sicilian. This practice of fabricating stories reflects the moral and narrative considerations in the *Klementia*, with Faustus also presenting a deceptive version of his own life story in *Klem.* 14, narrating his misfortunes from the perspective of "a friend" (cf. *Klem.* 14.7). This act of deception is absent in the *Recognitions*. Faustus lies to avoid recognition as a member of the imperial family and a return to a luxurious life without his family (*Klem.* 14.10). In 1904, Bousset remarked that no psychological motivation is given as to why Mattidia, Clement's as-of-yet unrecognized mother, chooses to deliberately deceive Peter.[255] However, Mattidia's deception stems from shame and a desire to protect her family and herself. Ashamed of her situation and the attempted affair by her brother-in-law, she flees to Athens, having fabricated a dream in front of her husband. Her lie serves as a form of *sophrosunè*, intended to prevent conflict between her husband and brother-in-law while simultaneously preserving her chastity.

When requested to recount her misfortunes, Mattidia engages in a disruptive narrative gesture by adopting, on an almost parasitically metanarrative level, the *persona* of a Greek heroine. This involves fiction within fiction, invoking love stories of novelistic protagonists from regions like Ephesus and Sicily, such as Xenophon's *Ephesiaca* and Chariton's novel set in Syracuse. This disrupts the expectations of the *Klementia*'s readers regarding the novelistic hypotext, already hinted at by other aforementioned fictional markers of Aradus and the temple setting. Moreover, this

---

[255] Bousset, "Die Wiedererkennungs-Fabel," 26–27.

act challenges the reader's perception of deceptive narratives, sparking curiosity not in the content itself, but in the interpretations of the stories told by Mattidia and later by Faustus, both of whom engage in fabrication. These fabrications evoke meta-literary reflection on the conventions of novelistic framework.

Mattidia actively crafts (*sophizein*) her own narrative as a novelistic account, inviting reflection on her *paideia* through her rhetorical control over the stories she tells. In this way, she contrasts with characters like Helen and Callirhoe, who are portrayed as victims of their beauty, with their misfortunes arousing the interest of poets and readers. Within the cluster of fictional markers that form the make-believe and by reflection on Mattidia as a metafictional Greek heroine avoiding this meta-narrative feeling of arousal, the reader is shown another significant aspect of the emphatic term associated with Mattidia, *aphellènisthènai*, involving a performance of *paideia* through *sophizein*.

Mattidia's act of *sophizein* (inventing) stories is motivated by *sophrosunè* and family honor. She does not transgress the boundaries of adultery, ambiguity, or other erotic matters. This stands in notable contrast, for example, with the pregnant Callirhoe, who also invents a story (σοφιζομένη) and tricks Dionysius into believing that she is pregnant with his child, in order to save her offspring (8.7.11). However, in the *Klementinist*'s eyes (*Klem.* 4.21), lying about the paternity of a child, particularly in connection with adulterous affairs, is morally unacceptable.

The moral ambiguity of novelistic heroines also lies in their use of ruses when they try to avoid marriage proposals by accepting them but also directly by postponing them under the pretence of wanting to wait until the right age or needing to resign from certain religious duties first (Xen. 3.11.4; Hld. 1.22.5–7). This feigning consent, though maintaining chastity towards their husband, can nevertheless be qualified as morally ambiguous. It reflects Aristotelian guidelines linking speech and intention with moral integrity and physical purity (*Rhet.* 2.6.21–22).[256] This becomes evident in Heliodorus' novel, where both Chariclea and Theagenes morally object to pretending to accept another lover's advances (Hld. 4.13.4; 7.21.5). In the *Klementia*, Mattidia does not even want to give any opportunity to think about (re)marrying, let alone the option of pretending acceptance.

Mattidia's *sophrosunè* and *eusebia* (piety or reverence towards the divine) provide her with *parrhèsia* (freedom of speech) and proper *paideia*. Unlike

---

[256] See also Augustine's *De Mendacio* §10; De Temmerman, *Crafting Characters*, 259–277.

the divine dreams in Heliodorus' *Aethiopica* (e.g., Kalasiris' dream from Apollo and Artemis, urging him to take Chariclea and Theagenes away from Delphi), Mattidia fabricates her own dream to maintain her moral and sexual integrity and to keep her own life story chaste. This reflects the moral truth underlying her deceptive storytelling as well as her use of the novelistic framework as a fictional device. This also contrasts with Helen's deceptive storytelling and ruses in the *Odyssey*.[257] In Book 4, Helen invites Telemachus, Peisistratus, and Menelaus to share stories after giving them some wine mixed with a drug to forget every trouble. She tells her version of the events at Troy, including how she recognized Odysseus, who had entered Troy disguised as a beggar, but she did not reveal his true identity. After all, she longed to return to her husband. Menelaus contradicts her rhetorical self-fashioning as a loving spouse, demonstrating how she tried to deceive the Greeks until the very end, even imitating the voices of the soldiers' wives to lure them out of the wooden horse (*Odyssey* 4.277–279). In other words, Helen endeavors to style herself as the heroine of her own *sophron* story, but fails due to moral ambiguity.

Mattidia represents a unique type of heroine, distinct not only from Helen and Greek novelistic heroines but also from figures such as Thecla from the *Apocryphal Acts of Paul and Thecla* and Justa from the *Conversion of Saint Cyprian*. These latter heroines – who also belong to the nobility – are converted by overhearing a preacher through an open window, without seeing him directly. This indirect encounter ignites in them the desire to see this preacher (*AAPTh* 7 and *The Conversion of Saint Cyprian* 1), which subtly evokes the motif of erotic desire typical of novelistic prose. This narrative device of conversion indoors serves to emphasize the virgin's modesty and chastity, contrasting similar scenes in non-Christian novelistic fiction, where the heroine's desire for the male protagonist arises from immediate physical attraction and love at first sight. In proposing this new form of desire, the *Acts* and hagiographical narratives advocate for a sex-negative morality, situating the heroine's longing in a literally confined space, removed from the ambiguities of physical attraction as characteristic of Greek adventure novels. Mattidia's conversion, in turn, does not occur through overheard teachings or within a confined interior (where she has to deal with her brother-in-law and her husband). Instead, she meets Peter in an open setting, even dominating him through her fictional storytelling. Her interaction with Peter repositions him not as a liberating preacher becoming the (eroticized) object of

---

[257] Cf. Praet, "Truth-telling, Lying and False Wisdom in the *Pseudo-Clementine*," 195–197.

the heroine's spiritualized love, but rather as a potential threat, perhaps even an unwelcome suitor in a public space.

Peter's *Encomium on Chastity* (*Klem.* 13.13–21)

Peter, after uncovering the deceptive nature of Mattidia's story, with its novelistic framework as mere – literally – fiction, nonetheless expresses confidence in her good intentions and supports her baptism. Her storytelling, coupled with her compassion for the sick woman she cares for, literally serves for Peter as the *hermeneutical* key (13.10: ἱκανὸν ἑρμηνέα) to her religious devotion and chastity. Hermeneutics not only guides the inquisitive Peter in interpreting her stories but also prompts, on a meta-literary level, the reader-*pepaideumenos* to engage, once again, with the meta-narrative aspects of *aphellènisthènai*. Mattidia represents a heroine of a new narrative discourse, distinct from erotic discourses and their heroines like Helen and Callirhoe.

Unique to the *Klementia*, this scene culminates in Peter's *Encomium on Chastity* or *sophrosunè*, demonstrating his rhetorical skill by employing a well-known rhetorical *progymnasma*. This *encomium* further underscores the meta-narrative reflections of the earlier passages in Aradus and reinforces several of the aforementioned aspects of *aphellènisthènai* regarding the discourse in which Mattidia emerges as the true *de-hellenized* heroine. While *Klem.* 13.13.1–13.14.1 parallels *Rec.* VII.38 in its focus on *sophrosunè*, the *Klementia* passage from 13.14.2 onwards uniquely elaborates upon the role of women in relation to chastity, deepening further meta-narrative reflections that, not coincidentally, tie closely with the fictional markers in Mattidia's recognition scene and the broader dynamics surrounding *aphellènisthènai*, the true heroine's discourse, and the readers' expectations.

The truly chaste heroine must prove herself to be an exemplary model for storytelling. Peter warns that any woman aspiring to be σώφρων will face cunning plots veiled under the pretext of love (προφάσει ἔρωτος) as a test. There is no place for adultery, erotic ambiguity, or remarriage (13.15), and the chaste woman must be aware of future punishment, while desiring the salvation of others. She thus becomes a literal model of a virtuous life (ἀγαθοῦ γὰρ βίου νόμος ἐστίν). As Peter elaborates on Mattidia's role, she emerges as the true subject and heroine of Christian storytelling,[258] wearing τοὺς σωφρονίζοντας λόγους (the words of chastity) like pearls: she allows no room for the affection of other men, except for her own husband, does not

---

[258] Cf. Calvet-Sébasti, "Femmes du roman pseudo-clémentin," 289.

engage in undisciplined laughter (γέλωτας ἀτάκτους), and regards all older men as potential threats (13.16.1–13.18.5).

Interestingly, the motif of wearing jewelry is significantly present in novelistic tradition. In Chariton's novel, Artaxates, the most trusted of the King's eunuchs, offers Callirhoe expensive jewelry (κόσμον πολυτελῆ, 6.5.4) to win her for his master. This motif, also present in non-novelistic traditions, persists in later Christian miracle narratives, such as those of Euphemia of Edessa and the Goth.[259] In the *Klementia*, however, the focus shifts to wearing chaste stories as the proper jewelled attire: unlike other narratives, there are no elaborate descriptions of suitors pursuing Mattidia or any resulting misfortunes.

Patricia Duncan argues that this *Klementinist encomium* is "awkwardly" inserted into the narrative context.[260] Her argument seems valid, as Peter addresses his *encomium* to the husband of such a chaste heroine, while Mattidia's husband is presumed dead at the moment. There is as yet no indication of an upcoming reunion with Faustus, which causes Mattidia's sobbing (13.20.1). This is indeed a striking passage. However, when viewed in light of its interaction with novelistic discourse and the accompanying meta-literary reflections of the preceding passage, it becomes evident that we are dealing here with further reflection, expressed by Peter's character, on the nature of moral novelistic literature and the *de-hellenizing* of its true heroine. Mattidia is not subjected to male gazes or erotic descriptions, and deities such as Eros and Aphrodite do not play a role. This discourse is unambiguous, contrasting narratives of heroines who remarry, are adorned by gifted jewels, or are defined by beauty and desire. Mattidia actively resists such discourses. True *sophrosunè* and fitting discourse are rooted in love of and for God, unlike, for instance, Chaereas' eulogy of Callirhoe's *sophrosunè* (6.12), which is ultimately attributed to the divine powers of Tuchè and Aphrodite.

Peter further insists that men must compel their wives to listen to such σεμνοὺς λόγους [*semnous logous*] (holy words), not to words that undermine chastity (13.17.1; 18.5). This may reflect broader commentary on how women should engage with Christian fiction rather than ambiguous Greek myths and narratives (cf. *Klem.* 5.25), which could include Greek novelistic prose. Notably, Mattidia is not subjected to such erotic gazing, and the reader is denied any opportunity to gaze upon her or indulge

---

[259] Premetaphrastic version section 8 and metaphrastic section 5; cf. Messis and Papaioannou, "Histoires 'gothiques'," 15–47; De Temmerman, "Callirhoe."
[260] Duncan, "Eve, Mattidia, and the Gender Discourse," 188.

in *ekphraseis* and comparisons. Our curiosity is not piqued in this area, unlike in works like those of Achilles Tatius, where sexual curiosity and ambiguity play a central role. A variant of this point can be found in the case of Melite, who captivates Cleitophon with her sexual allure, to which he, without resistance, reciprocates with overwhelming embraces and erotic desire (5.27.4).

Love needs no teaching other than his own, and is an admirable improviser; he can make any place a proper spot for the celebration of his mysteries. And as regards such enjoyment, that which has not been too carefully prepared is better far than the meticulously elaborated; it has in itself its own genuine and natural pleasure.	αὐτουργὸς γὰρ ὁ Ἔρως καὶ αὐτοσχέδιος σοφιστής, καὶ πάντα τόπον αὐτῷ τιθέμενος μυστήριον. τὸ δὲ ἀπερίεργον εἰς Ἀφροδίτην ἥδιον μᾶλλον τοῦ πολυπράγμονος· αὐτοφυῆ γὰρ ἔχει τὴν ἡδονήν.[261]

This passage manipulates the reader's expectations regarding erotic description, illustrating how the notion of *aperiergon* transcends into *polypragmon*. The readers are left free to fill in the gaps with their own imagination, as excessive description might spoil the experienced pleasure.[262] This ambiguous discourse contrasts with that of the *Klementia* and its heroine, Mattidia, reflecting on sexuality, morality, and authentic novelistic fiction in both form and content.

Desirous Gazing and Desirous Reading? *Encomium on Adultery* (*Klem.* 5)

The same underlying criticism appears in the fifth book of the *Klementia*, engaging more directly with another expression of Greek novelistic prose, notably Achilles Tatius' *Leucippe and Cleitophon*. This narrative was well-known among Christian authors,[263] which is also the case with the *Klementinist*.[264] In the *Encomium on Adultery* (*Klem.* 5.10–19), another highly original and profoundly Sophistic passage of the *Klementia*, erotic ambiguity and physical attraction are questioned. This passage connects with Peter's later *Encomium on Chastity* (*Klem.* 13), both engaging with the tradition of erotic novelistic prose. These passages, original to the

---

[261] Achilles Tatius, *Leucippe*, 302–303.
[262] Cf. Hunter, "The Curious Incident," 61–62.
[263] See Weinreich, *Der griechische Liebesroman*; Bremmer, "Achilles Tatius," 21–29.
[264] This is not noted by Weinreich, *Der griechische Liebesroman*.

Klementia, highlight the importance of novelistic engagement regarding the hermeneutics of reading the *Klementia* and interpreting its meta-narrative reflections.

The *Encomium on Adultery* (*Klem.* 5.10–19) forms part of a three-day discussion between Clement and the grammarian Appion, focusing on Clement's conversion and, more specifically, his critique of Greek *paideia* as immoral. Numerous myths of gods slaughtering one another, even devouring their own children, detrimentally influence the sexual and moral behavior of their audience, potential future *pepaideumenoi* (*Klem.* 4.7–21). Appion tries to reframe and hence preserve these myths as allegorical, natural philosophical, and thus ethically justifiable, truths.[265] This passage bears witness to the author's sophisticated rhetorical and philosophical background.[266] Previously considered as originating from a second-century Jewish-Alexandrian apologetical source,[267] its incorporation into the *Klementia* showcases its broader meta-narrative reflections, contributing to a broader hermeneutical framework throughout the narrative.

On the second day, Clement recalls a trick he once played on Appion in Rome. Feigning lovesickness, he prompted Appion to compose an *encomium* on adultery to persuade a Roman matrona to acquiesce to his advances. Appion cites various myths promoting adultery, arguing one should yield to the almighty Eros. However, not only is Clement not in love with any woman, but this woman does not exist at all. It is Clement himself who, by means of a letter, impersonates the matrona and refutes the immorality espoused by Appion and Greek culture in general. This passage exemplifies Greek *paideia,* employing rhetorical devices, engaging in playful references to Plato's *Phaedrus* and *Symposium*,[268] drawing on Neoplatonic philosophy,[269] and, important to our analysis here, expressions of novelistic prose. Among the elements refuted is the motif of the desiring gaze (*Klem.* 5.25.3–26.2): one should not look lasciviously upon another woman's beauty.

> And it behoves them also, before the springing of the desire, to satisfy the natural passion of puberty by marriage, first persuading them not to look upon the beauty of another woman (πρότερον πείσαντας εἰς εἶδος ἑτέρας γυναικὸς μὴ ἀτενίζειν). For our mind, whenever it is impressed

---

[265] Cf. De Vos, "The Disputes Between Appion and Clement," 81–109.
[266] Cf. Côté, "Les procédés rhétoriques," 189–210; De Vos, "The *Pseudo-Clementine* Lives."
[267] For a recent state-of-the-art, see De Vos, "The Role of the Homilistic Disputes," 54–88.
[268] Cf. De Vos, "Plato's Phaedrus and Symposium in the Pseudo-Clementine Homilies," 102–146.
[269] Cf. Côté, "La théogonie orphique," 85–122.

delightfully with the image of a beloved one (ὁπόταν τὰ πρῶτα τῇ τέρψει τὸ εἶδος τῆς ἐρωμένης ἀπομάξηται), always seeing the form as in a mirror (ὥσπερ ἐν κατόπτρῳ ἐνορῶν ἀεὶ τὴν μορφήν), is tormented by the recollection (διὰ τῆς μνήμης βασανίζεται); and if it do not obtain its desire, it contrives ways of obtaining it.[270]

The matrona's complaint remarkably mirrors Cleitophon's description in 5.13.3–4, when Leucippe is believed to be dead and Melite becomes consumed with love for Cleitophon: she cannot eat and perpetually gazes at him, while Cleitophon perceives her erotic and desirous glance and describes it from her perspective:

She did nothing but gaze upon me. To lovers there is no delight save in the object of love, which occupies the whole of their soul, and leaves no place in it for the pleasures of the table. The pleasure which comes from vision enters by the eyes and makes its home in the breast; bearing with it ever the image of the beloved, it impresses it upon the mirror of the soul and leaves there its image; the emanation given off by beauty travels by invisible rays to the lovesick heart and imprints upon it its *silhouette*.	πάντα δὲ ἔβλεπεν ἐμέ. οὐδὲν γὰρ ἡδὺ τοῖς ἐρῶσι πλὴν τὸ ἐρώμενον· τὴν γὰρ ψυχὴν πᾶσαν ὁ ἔρως καταλαβών, οὐδὲ αὐτῇ χώραν δίδωσι τῇ τροφῇ. ἡ δὲ τῆς θέας ἡδονὴ διὰ τῶν ὀμμάτων εἰσρέουσα τοῖς στέρνοις ἐγκάθηται· ἕλκουσα δὲ τοῦ ἐρωμένου τὸ εἴδωλον ἀεί, ἐναπομάττεται τῷ τῆς ψυχῆς κατόπτρῳ καὶ ἀναπλάττει τὴν μορφήν· ἡ δὲ τοῦ κάλλους ἀπορροὴ δι' ἀφανῶν ἀκτίνων ἐπὶ τὴν ἐρωτικὴν ἑλκομένη καρδίαν ἐναποσφραγίζει κάτω τὴν σκιάν.[271]

The desirous gaze is questioned as part of an ambiguous discourse; one should not gaze upon another's beauty.[272] Both Melite and Cleitophon falter: Melite succumbs to desire, and Cleitophon, in turn, allows her desirous gaze, unlike the chaste heroine lauded by Peter in his *Encomium on Chastity* (*Klem.* 13). In the *Klementia*, the matrona and Clement employ similar, at times even identical, terminology to articulate the process of gazing upon the beloved's beauty, with terms like *τέρψει* (*Klem.*) and ἡδύ (A.T. [Achilles Tatius]), evoking the impression that the image leaves (*Klem. ἀπομάξηται*; A.T. *ἐναπομάττεται*) upon the mirror of the soul

---

[270] Roberts and Donaldson, *Ante-Nicene Christian Library Vol. XVII*, 113; Rehm and Strecker, *Pseudoklementinen I*, 102–103.
[271] Achilles Tatius, *Leucippe*, 145–146.
[272] Erotic tensions and feelings of love in a convivial setting was a popular motif in novelistic works; cf. Hld. 3.11; Chariton 2.4 and 4.5; *Hist. Apol.* section 17; Achilles Tatius 1.5.3; and the *Sesonchosis*-fragment P.Oxy.3319 (Col. 3, 17–23).

(A.T. τῷ τῆς ψυχῆς κατόπτρῳ) or within the mind as if reflected in a mirror (*Klem.* ὥσπερ ἐν κατόπτρῳ). The form (*Klem.* τὴν μορφήν; A.T. τὴν μορφήν) is hence indelibly imprinted into the lover's heart or memory.

Scholars of ancient narrative have already acknowledged the erotic significance of visuality (in combination with physical beauty) in novelistic prose, especially in Achilles Tatius.[273] In a well-known passage, Achilles describes the birth of desire as a response to visual stimuli; this is exemplified in Cleitophon's vivid first-person account of his infatuation with Leucippe: "the eye is the passage for love's wound (ὀφθαλμὸς γὰρ ὁδὸς ἐρωτικῷ τραύματι; 1.4.4)."[274] This dynamic contrasts Callirhoe, objectified by erotic gazing, with Mattidia, who eludes it. Erotic gazing, which forms part of ambivalent imagery and erotically implicit rhetoric within novelistic contexts, is critiqued within the *Klementia* and clearly linked to one's Greek status. Not coincidentally, in *Klem.* 4–6 we find a broader discussion about Greek *paideia*, the spectrum of Greekness, the status of *pepaideumenos*, and the process of *aphellēnisthēnai*, which neatly connects with Mattidia's recognition scene and meta-narrative dynamics regarding *aphellēnizesthai*.

This meta-literary idea has further implications for the *Klementia* as Christian fiction. Adventures and the fascination to uncover all (grotesque) details, as typical for novelistic expressions, are replaced by succinct testimonies, with tantalizing details, ambiguous physiognomic descriptions, and lustful gazes notably absent. The *Klementia* reconfigures the flexible boundaries of Greek novelistic discourse, offering an alternative, *de-hellenized* way of experiencing beauty within a framework Peter refers to as *semnoi logoi*. This shift, on a higher level, reflects how a *pepaideumenos* is expected to engage with both *Klementinist* discourse and other expressions of Greek novelistic prose, highlighting the confrontational significance of *aphellēnisthēnai* in relation to cultural, literary, and moral terms, and what it means (or does not mean) to read prose fiction as a Greek *pepaideumenos*.

The Hermeneutics of the Reader's Identity:
Ἀφελληνισθῆναι *(Aphellēnisthēnai) as Re-hellenization*

Reading strategies are key to the *Klementia*, with its layered storytelling inviting readers to engage deeply with its moral and cultural implications. The recognition scenes are not merely "entertainment" value, but require a concerted effort to fathom the hermeneutical layering embedded within the narrative. Readers are implicitly invited to identify the

---

[273] Cf. Morales, *Vision and Narrative*.
[274] Achilles Tatius, *Leucippe*, 14–15.

multiple fictional markers and reflect on accompanying moral and cultural considerations, however, from within their position as cultural Greeks. This interaction highlights the tension between maintaining Greek identity and the *de-hellenizing* of novelistic discourse. The concept of *aphellènisthènai* brings significant tensions: readers are validated in their Greek cultural role through their recognition of the strategies of make-believe, but at the same time compelled to reconsider the *de-hellenizing*, renegotiated boundaries of novelistic discourse. In this regard, the *Klementia*, as unique, late-ancient, and self-reflexive fiction, redefines how one ought to *learn to read* as a *pepaideumenos*. The processes of *hellenizein* and *aphellènizesthai* are integral to the hermeneutics of interpretation, including hypertextual references, alongside reflections offered by Peter (*Klem.* 13) and Clement (*Klem.* 5) on novelistic discourse and storytelling. These hermeneutical dynamics reveal a striking tension: *de-hellenization* simultaneously operates as a form of *re-hellenization*, in an intense and perhaps even painful act, pushing the reader to affirm the dynamics of make-believe from within Greek *paideia* as *habitus*.

This discussion ties in to our earlier considerations on *hellènizein* and *aphellènizesthai*, focusing on how one becomes culturally Greek through continuous, repetitive action and behavior. The *Klementia* articulates a voice that can only be understood within this cultural framework of identity formation and Greek *paideia*. Much like Favorinus, a self-declared paragon of accomplished Greekness for the Corinthians striving to become Greek (again) through a painstaking process, Mattidia undergoes a similar, but reversed (and even meta-narrative), process well before her conversion by Peter. She has already distanced herself from other ambiguous erotic and novelistic discourses typical of Greek heroines, effectively embodying an *anima naturaliter Christiana* as a stern and chaste Roman woman, which caused her to refute her brother-in-law's advances. This represents an important step towards salvation and re-evaluation of what it means (not) to be culturally Greek. Alongside our earlier reflections on the Greekness of the reader and the triggers of make-believe, we observe several centripetal, but predominantly centrifugal dynamics concerning Greek identity. The *Klementinist* engages readers with sophisticated philosophical, literary, and rhetorical capital, extending beyond mere adherence to purity laws or simple conviction and conversion by the Christian content of the narrative. The reader is frequently confronted with the hermeneutical act of reading "truth": moral truth, philosophical truth, and the truth of stories. I argue that reading this narrative constitutes a sociocultural act, foregrounding and reconsidering one's identity as a redefined reader-*pepaideumenos* and reassessing the true moral and cultural value of novelistic discourse.

The meta-narrative connections and hermeneutical strategies concerning novelistic prose, and how the *implied reader* engages through their position as cultural Greek, form part of a broader discourse of intellectual games and deceptive frameworks deployed in the *Klementia*.[275] For example, during the discussion on *paideia* and Clement's critique of it in *Klem.* 4–6, Clement deceives the grammarian Appion through a sophisticated ploy of rhetorical *dissimulation* and deceptive *ethopoeia* (an ancient rhetorical concept indicating the technique of creating an imaginary speech of a real or mythical person). This is not so much a conflict rooted in anti-Judaism, but rather a contest steeped in Greek *paideia*, despite Clement's criticism of *paideia*. Moreover, Mattidia also flirts with deception in her interaction with Peter, taking on a fictional novelistic framework.

This begs the question of the reader's role and the nature of the engagement with fictional complicity: is, as past scholarship has suggested, the goal straightforward conversion or an apology, or is the *Pseudo-Clementine* literature a manual for catechumens,[276] meant to refute pagan philosophers?[277] I argue that the *Klementia*'s meta-reflections on *paideia* transcend this singular, straightforward goal. Its meta-narrative techniques prompt the reader to explore the boundaries of truth, engaging with shared capital of *paideia* and re-establishing one's role as *pepaideumenos*. These redefined *pepaideumenoi* are continually tested in their erudition throughout the novel regarding hermeneutical strategies for interpreting Gospel traditions, Scriptures, Plato's dialogues, particularly his myths, and various expressions of novelistic discourse.

Stanley Jones provocatively suggests that the *Klementia* functions as a non-idealistic novel or even an "outlandish parody," as "comic elements grab the upper hand [such as the face-swap scene or the theory of false pericopes]."[278] Jones even likens the *Klementinist* to a fourth-century Judaizing Christian Mel Brooks, who transforms every character into "a buffoon, even Peter."[279] It warrants deeper examination to determine whether all these elements indeed constitute part of a parodic discourse. In my view, such an interpretation may be overly simplistic. Additionally, the concept of "idealistic," "realistic," and potential "parodic" novels should be

---

[275] Cf. De Vos, "The Pseudo-Clementine Homilies and the Art of 'Fake News'," 423–459.
[276] Cf. Waitz, *Die Pseudoklementinen*, 48, 50.
[277] Cf. Teeple, *The Prophet in the Clementines*.
[278] Jones, "Novels," 296 and 299–300.
[279] Jones, "The Identities of the Pseudo-Clementine Authors," 9.

reconsidered.²⁸⁰ Nevertheless, it is notable that, as I have argued, themes of deception, dissimulation, and truth play a central role in the *Klementia*, where the *Klementinist* displays *paideia,* encouraging readers to reflect on both *paideia* itself and the challenges of being a *pepaideumenos*.

Ἀφελληνισθῆναι *(Aphellênisthênai)* and the Dynamics of Sophistic Christianity

A point to consider is the extent to which this discourse can be called "Christian." While the *Klementia* is undoubtedly a religious–philosophical novel, the decentralizing reflections on Greek identity and the process of (de-)hellenization should also be understood as emerging from within the Greek *paideutic* frameworks. It engages with the aforementioned spectrum of Greekness, a dynamic process also significant among Christians as *pepaideumenoi*. This dialectical engagement with Greekness appears in other non-Christian literary testimonies, with which the *Klementia* demonstrates numerous interesting similarities, including certain literary–philosophical expressions from the Second Sophistic and the notion of paradoxical *paideia*.²⁸¹

A rather harsh, ironic, and paradoxical form of *paideia* has been highlighted by William Adler, who examined the aforementioned *Apion section* (*Klem.* 4–6) as a satirical play on Greek rhetorical and philosophical traditions, intertwined with playful intertextuality involving the then widespread *Antiochus narrative*.²⁸² The section indeed represents a multilayered interplay of deception and dissimulation. As previously noted, Appion, drawing on Greek *paideia*, offers an *encomium* (paradoxically praising adultery), a rhetorical exercise well established in Greek rhetorical education,²⁸³ citing examples from Greek mythology and philosophy (cf. *Klem.* 5.18). Later, within the disputes in Tyre, Clement uses this *encomium* as an example of the moral corruption inherent in Greek *paideia*. However, this is far from a simple refutation – it is a deeply sophisticated one. Clement entirely fabricates his lovesickness. The letter he cites is fictional, with the "response" to, or rather a rebuttal of, this encomiastic letter supposedly from a Roman matrona – depicted as a converted Jewish matron-philosopher – who is actually Clement himself in disguise. Thus, Clement is portrayed as deliberately leveraging his training in Greek *paideia*, crafting speeches and personas of, in this case, fictitious characters as part of the known Greek rhetorical exercise of *ethopoeia*.

---

²⁸⁰ Cf. De Temmerman, "Chaereas Revisited," 247–262.
²⁸¹ For a general discussion of paradoxical *paideia*, see Anderson, *The Second Sophistic*, 51ff.
²⁸² Adler, "Apion's 'Encomium of Adultery'," 15–49.
²⁸³ Cf. Kennedy, *Progymnasmata*, 50.

This form of *paradoxical paideia* can best be understood within the broader context of the Sophistic movement. Adler and Carleton Paget suggest that *Klem.* 4–6 derives from a second-century text with Sophistic pretensions, later inserted into the *Klementinist* narrative.[284] However, recognizing Sophistic elements of paradoxical *paideia* within the *Klementia* does not require this theory. Consider, for instance, the imaginative literary epistolography, a minor genre of the Second Sophistic.[285] These Sophistic interests should also be considered in relation to *Klementia*'s engagement with other expressions of the Sophistic movement, including Greek novels such as Achilles Tatius' *Leucippe and Cleitophon*. Although I avoid labelling the work a "Sophistic" novel, as Ruth Webb cautions regarding Achilles and Heliodorus,[286] and do not endorse Chapman's suggestion that the *Pseudo-Clementine* author was a former Sophist,[287] I do position the *Klementinist* within a dynamic environment of *paideutic* and *Sophistic* reflections, as we can also see in Greek novels, on Greek identity and processes of Greekness and *de-hellenization*.

Therefore, the *Klementia* provides valuable insights into the complex relationship between Christian and Sophistic strategies of identity construction and literary production. Recent scholarship has explored Christian figures such as the second-century Tatian within a Sophistic context,[288] highlighting the relationship between Christian literature and the cultural milieu of the Second Sophistic and Late Antiquity. Scott Fitzgerald Johnson remarked that Christian apocryphal literature, coining it the "dark matter" of this period, nevertheless remains neglected amidst the otherwise intensely studied postclassical literature and topics like minority identity.[289]

The *Klementia* deserves further scholarly attention for its role in this context. Exploring its aims and literary qualities can nuance Jones' recent statement and Chapman's view of the *Pseudo-Clementine* author as an ex-Sophist, while also adding nuance to Franz Boll's influential perspective. Boll suggested a connection between Clement's dissatisfaction with philosophical schools, already found in the *Grundschrift*, and Lucian's *Piscator* or *Menippus*, but argued that the *Grundschrift* author, due to the serious

---

[284] Adler, "Apion's 'Encomium of Adultery'"; Carleton Paget, *Jews*, 466–467.
[285] Kennedy, *Progymnasmata*, 47–48, n149.
[286] Webb, "Rhetoric and the Novel," 527.
[287] Chapman, "On the Date of the Clementines," 147–159.
[288] Cf. Nasrallah, "Mapping the World," 283–314; for the role of *paideia* and Second Sophistic in Tatian's work, see Timotin, "Σοφία barbare," 553–574.
[289] Johnson, "Christian Apocrypha," 669.

tone (*Ernst*) of the work, could not (*unwahrscheinlicher Weise*) have drawn directly from the humorous Lucian.[290]

While I do not claim that the *Basic Writer* or *Klementinist* directly used Lucian's work, I argue that the *Klementinist*, unlike the *Recognitionist* or the author of the Syriac version, developed unique paradoxical reflections on *paideia*. While these may have been present in the *Grundschrift*, they are elaborated distinctively in the *Klementia*. To fully appreciate these dynamics, it is essential to consider the *Klementinist*'s engagement with *paideia*, Greek identity, and the broader intellectual currents of the Second Sophistic, to which also Lucian and Favorinus belonged. Additionally, Laurent Pernot's concept of the "Third Sophistic" or "Second Sophistic Encored" in the fourth century is also relevant, as "sophistic figures continued to flourish in the Christian empire, in the world of Late Antiquity, presenting the characteristics as before and still displaying a combination of literature and politics under rhetoric's auspices."[291]

The *Klementia* offers a sophisticated approach to late-ancient rhetorical, literary, and philosophical "capital," rather than simply refuting "Greeks" and Greek *paideia* and defending "Jewish" identity, customs, and laws. These identities are deeply interwoven with reflections on *paideutic* capital. We observe a cultural continuity, with *paideia* engaged in creative, sometimes ironic, or even paradoxical ways. Conversely, *paideia* serves a deconstructive and centripetal function, as it is not only fiercely criticized but also dissected explicitly and implicitly by the *Klementinist*. This aligns with recent scholarly appraisals of Sophistic and late-ancient dynamics of inclusion, exclusion, and modes of self-presentation concerning the *paideia* of early Christian authors and readers.

Some Concluding Reflections on Future Scholarship

The *Klementia* merits recognition as a Christian and *paideutic* witness reflecting on both centripetal and centrifugal aspects of Greek cultural identity and literature. Cases of Sophistic and paradoxical *paideia*, along with strategies of make-believe and erotic novelistic fiction, exemplify this. Future *Pseudo-Clementine* scholarship should evidently focus on exploring the various *Pseudo-Clementines* expressions as original fiction, examining how strategies of fictionality and readership expectations are shaped within a broader literary, Sophistic, and philosophical environment.

---

[290] Boll, "Das Eingangsstück der Ps.-Klementinen," 140.
[291] Pernot, "Greek and Latin Rhetorical Culture," 212; cf. Pernot, "The Concept of a Third Sophistic," 177–187.

This Element encourages further studies on the *Klementia* and other *Pseudo-Clementine* traditions as Christian fiction revealing unique late-ancient cultural and moral reflections on the writing and reading of fiction.

The comparative analysis with Chariton's and Achilles Tatius' novels has proven insightful, but the relationship to Heliodorus' *Aethiopica* also merits exploration. Dirk Uwe Hansen assumed that the *Aethiopica* influenced the *Grundschrift*, considering it an older novel.[292] Today, it is generally accepted that Heliodorus' work dates to the fourth century,[293] ranking it as an even younger work than the *Klementia*. In any case, both texts present moral and meta-literary hermeneutics that may indicate shared or interconnected cultural frameworks and literary interests. As in the *Klementia*, the contours of the heroine's chastity in the *Aethiopica* are emphasized more strictly than in earlier Greek and Latin novelistic prose, but while the *Aethiopica* emphasizes virginity before marriage, the *Klementia* centers on sex-positive chastity within marriage. As Montiglio noted,[294] the *Aethiopica* affords the reader less opportunity to commit acts of curious, desirous, and adulterous looking.[295] Chastity underpins discussions of true beauty (e.g., 5.14.1–2), framing a meta-narrative framework about beauty and ambiguous *sophrosunè* for readers. Rather than interpreting this as direct interaction, we ought to examine it as an instance of *paideutic* and literary expression reflecting a similar *Zeitgeist*, along with cultural and moral reflections regarding writing and reading strategies.

Moreover, Heliodorus' novel and the *Klementia* exhibit shared interpretations of centrifugal and centripetal strategies regarding the spectrum of Greek cultural identity. In the *Aethiopica*, "[t]he constructed and unstable nature of cultural identity plays an important role."[296] The interplay between local (Ethiopian) and more universal (Greek) cultural identities, alongside the lineage of nobility, is central to the *Aethiopica*, culminating in the Greek Ethiopian protagonist's reintegration into Ethiopian society. The story is not merely about the loss and restitution of Greek identity, as experienced by other Greek novelistic heroines. Instead, it reveals more profound but also manipulative dynamics regarding cultural identity. For example, the local elite speaks Greek, and Calasiris recites a biography of

---

[292] Hansen, "Die Metamorphose des Heiligen Clemens," 119–129.
[293] Cf. Keydell, "Zur Datierung der *Aithiopika*," 345–350.
[294] Montiglio, "Chariclea's Beauty."
[295] See also Konstan, *Sexual Symmetry*; Goldhill, *Foucault's Virginity*.
[296] Kruchió, "Heliodorus."

Homer, who would be an Egyptian wanderer and with whom Calasiris assimilates his own life, blending Egyptian wisdom with Greek aspects.[297]

The *Klementia* and *Aethiopica* share concerns about cultural identity, fictional strategies, and hermeneutics of interpreting the novels as a (redefined) cultural Greek or *pepaideumenos*. The *Klementia* explores Greekness in relation to the Roman background of Mattidia and her family, who are related to the very Emperor himself. Unlike earlier novels where the heroine seeks restitution as a Greek, the protagonist engages in a profound dialogue between Greekness, *Romanitas*, and expressions of Christian religion within the broader Eastern Mediterranean cultural framework. This dialogue culminates in a familial reunion within a Christian framework rather than a restitution of a Greek couple. Understanding these hermeneutic strategies of fictionality requires examining "Greekness," cultural identity, and literary production regarding the *Klementia* as well as the *Aethiopica*, highlighting their relevance to ancient narrative, Christian fiction, and cultural identity. Moreover, a crucial, yet underexamined, distinction with the Latin *Recognitions* of Rufinus emerges here.

Make Clement Roman Again

In the prologue to his early fifth-century *Recognitions*, Rufinus of Aquileia expresses his intent to restore Clement to his Roman roots. He addresses Bishop Gaudentius to receive Clement's story as no small spoil (*praedam non parvam*) and, above all, as Roman (*suscipe iam Romanum*).[298] Dominique Côté interprets this rendering of Clement as *Romanus* not only as a political–ecclesiastical claim to authority by the Latin-speaking Roman Church, but also as part of a discussion between Rufinus and Jerome regarding *paideia* and the educated Christian.[299] In his *Apology against Jerome* (2.7), Rufinus criticizes Jerome in his classical *paideia* and his ambition to Christianize foreign knowledge by, among other things, incorporating quotes from Greek sources.

Building on Côté's view of Rufinus' attitude towards *paideia*, I suggest that this reflects even more complex dynamics concerning the hermeneutics of interpretation and the reader's formation regarding cultural identity. While within the framework of *aphellènisthènai*, the *Klementia* originally features strategies of curiosity, instances of dissimulation, expressions of Sophistic and paradoxical *paideia*, and cases of (hypertextual and/or meta-literary)

---

[297] Think also of Indian gymnosophists who speak Greek perfectly in Philostratus' *Vita Apollonii* (Book 6).
[298] Rehm and Strecker, *Pseudoklementinen II*, 3–4.
[299] Côté, "Rufinus of Aquileia and the Reception of the *Recognitions*."

interaction with Greek novelistic prose, they are largely absent in Rufinus' *Recognitions*.[300] This raises questions about Rufinus' role in this absence and how his attempt to restore Clement relates to Roman identity and the centripetal and centrifugal dynamics regarding Greek cultural identity, *Romanitas*, and literary production.

Pseudo-Clementines as Philosophy

This manifests in the realm of philosophy and the various ways fiction and philosophy enrich one another in the *Klementia* and *Recognitions*. In the future, I shall elaborate not only on how the *Klementia* reflects upon philosophy and *paideia* and engages with fourth-century philosophical dialogues, addressing both Christian and non-Christian, particularly Neoplatonic, philosophers, the Sophistic environment, and accompanying interests in medicinal knowledge,[301] but also on how the *Recognitions* engages with philosophy in a distinct manner, specifically regarding Plato. The interaction with Plato in the *Klementia* demonstrates a sophisticated approach, treating fiction in an exceptional way. As previously noted, the hypotext of the Myth of Er in Faustus' recognition scene invites meta-literary reflections on literary discourses, philosophical myths, and readers' experiences regarding "truth." Recently, I discussed reflections on the truth of philosophical rhetoric, oral dialectics, and the function of lies as moral truths in the *Klementia*, notably in Apion's *Encomium on Adultery* and the introductory letters, which constitute an interaction with Plato's *Symposium* and *Phaedrus*. These reflections, prompted by intertextual links with Plato's dialogues, encourage the reader to contemplate rhetoric, dialectics, and irony.[302]

The originality of philosophical capital in the *Recognitions* remains underexplored. Nevertheless, it is evident that we are also dealing with an original philosophical novel that presents a Christian, philosophical way of life attached to Clement's life story. Furthermore, the *Recognitions* approaches the concept of "lived philosophy" distinctively: the reception of well-known Platonic images such as the Allegory of the Cave and the Charioteer myth, as well as familiar quotations, are not mere incidental references; they form part of the broader philosophical–narrative arc within the *Recognitions*, Clement's philosophical quest, and the discourse of Peter and his followers regarding lived (Christian) philosophy. Through

---

[300] Regarding the motifs of deception and dissimulation, cf. De Vos, "The Pseudo-Clementine Homilies and the Art of 'Fake News'."
[301] Cf. De Vos, "The *Pseudo-Clementine* Lives."
[302] De Vos, "Plato's Phaedrus and Symposium in the Pseudo-Clementine Homilies," 102–146.

various reinterpretations of Platonic philosophy, Peter delves deeper into a Christian perspective on the late-ancient philosophical program of ethics, physics, logic, and metaphysics, connected to the lives of Clement and his family. Here, the originality of Christian philosophy in relation to the literary framework of the *Recognitions* becomes apparent.[303]

Additionally, the later reception of the *Recognitions* as a philosophical work is still significantly underexplored, despite its profound impact not only as a literary narrative on subsequent Western literature but also due to its philosophical capital. Particularly notable is that the *Recognitions* was perceived as a repository of non-Christian *paideia*. Glossaries such as the ninth-century Leyden Glossary (Vossianus lat. Q.69, for. 32v–33r) and the eleventh-century *Bibliotheca Ambrosiana 79 Sup.*, fols. 127r–v, refer to the *Recognitions* as a container of philosophical traditions. These glosses trace back to a tradition that began in the so-called Canterbury School, under Theodorus of Tarsus (602–690), Archbishop of Canterbury from 668 to 690, and Hadrianus of Nisida (before 637–ca. 709), Abbot of the Monastery of St. Peter and St. Paul.[304] In addition to interests in Augustine, Cassian, and Isidore of Seville, there was also an interest in classical literature and the *Pseudo-Clementine Recognitions* as part of the educational program. This warrants further scholarly exploration to fully comprehend the rich world of the *Pseudo-Clementines*, as there are also Syrian and Arabic *Pseudo-Clementine* traditions that largely remain uncharted territory, particularly regarding *paideia* and philosophy.[305]

Klementia's *Nachleben* (Afterlife)

And rich it is! We possess a highly fluid *Pseudo-Clementine* literary world offering deeper insight into strategies of fictionality and accompanying reflections on morality and cultural identity, as well as the hermeneutics of reading and writing that have changed over time. Moreover, the *Klementia* and *Recognitions* have been of great influence on later Western narrative traditions.[306]

---

[303] Cf. De Vos, "The *Pseudo-Clementine Recognitions* as Early Christian Philosophy."
[304] Hawk, "The Pseudo-Clementines and the Canterbury School."
[305] For a fundamental first step regarding the Arabic traditions and the relationship between philosophy and fiction, see DiRusso, "From Mournful Mattidia to Mitradora the Philosopher."
[306] The *Recognitions* were printed earlier than the *Klementia*, in 1504 in Paris, by Jacobus Faber Stapulensis. The diffusion of the *Recognitions* was also important in Western-European regions, since ca. 115 manuscripts have been preserved (dating between the sixth and fifteenth centuries, in Italy, France, Germany, the British Isles, and Iceland); cf. Svennung, "Handschriften zu den pseudoklementinischen Recognitiones," 473–476.

Two traditions of epitomes of the *Klementia* exist: the younger epitome (e) or *jüngere* or *metaphrastische Epitome*,[307] edited by Symeon the Metaphrast in the tenth century, and the older epitome (E) or *vormetaphrastische Epitome*, presumably from the fifth-sixth century, which features dogmatic alterations and narrative adjustments.[308] Epitome (e) is likely based on (E). Both epitomes circulated widely, with 190 extant witnesses, and were printed in 1555 by Hadrianus Turnebus in Paris, before the original *Klementia* were printed. Bernard Pouderon also mentions a third kind of epitome: the *Historia Fausti* or *De Fausto*, found in a sixteenth-seventeenth-century manuscript (*Bodleianus lib. Holkham gr.58, fol. 303v–307v*).[309] This epitome, based on epitome (e), significantly influenced the Doctor Faust legends. Scholarship has already noted an indirect influence of Simon Magus' character and the *Pseudo-Clementine* corpus on Faustian traditions; this connection should not surprise us: just as Clement embarks upon a search for truth at the outset of his autobiography, Doctor Faust similarly embarks upon a search for knowledge, grappling with illusions, necromancy, conjuring up Helen of Troy herself, similar to Simon Magus in the *Klementia*. While their behaviors differ, this connection offers valuable philosophical and theological perspectives, captivating modern readers and unveiling the early Christian roots of one of the most important narratives in Western culture that has yet to reveal all of its secrets.[310]

---

[307] Dressel, *Clementis Romani*; Rehm and Strecker, *Pseudoklementinen I*, xiv–xvi.
[308] Cf. Paschke, *Die beiden griechischen Klementinen-Epitomen*; Risch, *Die Pseudoklementinen IV: Die Klemens-Biographie*.
[309] Pouderon, "Faust, le *Faustbuch* et le Faustus Pseudo-Clémentin," 127–148.
[310] Cf. Pouderon, *Métamorphoses de Simon le magicien*.

Bibliography

Achilles Tatius. *Leucippe and Clitophon* (translated by Stephen Gaselee). Cambridge: Harvard University Press, 1969.
Adler, William. "Apion's 'Encomium of Adultery': A Jewish Satire of Greek Paideia in the Pseudo-Clementine *Homilies*," *Hebrew Union College Annual* 64 (1993): 15–49.
Allen, Graham. *Intertextuality: The New Critical Idiom*. Abingdon: Routledge, 2022.
Amsler, Frédéric. "État de la recherche récente sur le roman pseudo-clémentin," in *Nouvelles intrigues pseudo-clémentines. Actes du deuxième colloque international sur la littérature apocryphe chrétienne, Lausanne–Genève, 30 août–2 septembre 2006*. Frédéric Amsler, et al., eds. Prahins: Éditions du Zèbre, 2008a, 25–45.
Amsler, Frédéric. "Peter and His Secretary in Pseudo-Clement," in *Writing the Bible: Scribes, Scribalism and Script*. Philip R. Davies and Thomas Römer, eds. London-New York: Routledge–Taylor & Francis Group, 2013, 177–188.
Amsler, Frédéric, Frey, Albert, and Touati, Charlotte, eds. *Nouvelles intrigues pseudo-clémentines. Actes du deuxième colloque international sur la littérature apocryphe chrétienne, Lausanne–Genève, 30 août–2 septembre 2006*. Prahins: Éditions du Zèbre, 2008.
Anderson, Graham. "The Pepaideumenos in Action: Sophists and Their Outlook in the Early Empire," *ANRW 2.33.1* 6 (1989): 79–208.
Anderson, Graham. *The Second Sophistic: A Cultural Phenomenon in the Roman Empire*. London: Routledge, 1993.
Baldick, Chris. "Implied Reader," in *The Concise Oxford Dictionary of Literary Terms*. Chris Baldick, ed. Oxford: Oxford University Press, 2001, 123.
Basso, Sergio. "*Homilies*, Hermogenes and Syriac Exegesis," in *In Search of Truth in the Pseudo-Clementine Homilies: New Approaches to a Philosophical and Rhetorical Novel of Late Antiquity*. B. M. J. De Vos and D. Praet, eds. Tübingen: Mohr Siebeck, 2022, 107–129.
Baur, Ferdinand Christian. "Die Christuspartei in der korinthischen Gemeinde, der Gegensatz des petrinischen und paulinischen Christentums in der ältesten Kirche, der Apostel Petrus in Rom," *Tübinger Zeitschrift für Theologie* 3.4 (1831): 61–206.
Baur, Ferdinand Christian. *Die christliche Gnosis oder die christliche Religions-Philosophie in ihrer geschichtlichen Entwicklung*. Tübingen: C. F. Osiander, 1835.

Bazzana, Giovanni Battista. "Eve, Cain, and the Giants: The Female Prophetic Principle and Its Succession in the Pseudo-Clementine Novel," in *Nouvelles intrigues pseudo-clémentines: Actes du deuxième colloque international sur la littérature apocryphe chrétienne, Lausanne–Genève, 30 août-2 septembre 2006*. Frédéric Amsler et al., eds. Prahins: Éditions du Zèbre, 2008, 313–320.

Bigg, Charles. "The Clementine Homilies," *Studia Biblica et Ecclesiastica* 2 (1890): 157–193.

Boll, Franz. "Das Eingangsstück der Ps.-Klementinen," *Zeitschrift für die neutestamentliche Wissenschaft* 17 (1916): 139–148.

Bolyki, János. "Recognitions in the Pseudo-Clementina," in *The Pseudo-Clementines*. Jan N. Bremmer, ed. Leuven: Peeters, 2010, 191–199.

Borg, Barbara. *Paideia: The World of the Second Sophistic*. Berlin-New York: De Gruyter, 2004.

Bossu, Annelies. "Steadfast and Shrewd Heroines: The Defence of Chastity in the Latin Post-Nicene Passions and the Greek Novels," *Ancient Narrative* 12 (2015): 91–128.

Bossu, Annelies, De Temmerman, Koen, and Praet, Danny. "The Saint as Cunning Heroine: Rhetoric and Characterization in the Passio Caeciliae," *Mnemosyne* 69.3 (2016): 433–452.

Boulhol, Pascal. "La conversion de l'anagnorismos profane dans le roman pseudo-clémentin," in *Nouvelles intrigues pseudo-clémentines. Actes du deuxième colloque international sur la littérature apocryphe chrétienne, Lausanne–Genève, 30 août-2 septembre 2006*. Frédéric Amsler et al., eds. Prahins: Éditions du Zèbre, 2008, 151–175.

Bourdieu, Pierre. *Les règles de l'art. Genèse et structure du champ littéraire*. Paris: Éditions du Seuil, 1992.

Bousset, Wilhelm. "Die Wiedererkennungs-Fabel in den pseudoklementinischen Schriften, den Menächmen des Plautus und Shakespeares Komödie der Irrungen," *Zeitschrift für die neutestamentliche Wissenschaft und die Kunde der älteren Kirche* 5 (1904): 18–27.

Bousset, Wilhelm. "Die Geschichte eines Wiedererkennungsmärchens," *Nachrichten von der Gesellschaft der Wissenschaften zu Göttingen. Philologisch-historische Klasse* (1916): 469–551.

Bovon, François. "En tête des Homélies clémentines: La lettre de Pierre à Jacques," in *Nouvelles intrigues pseudo-clémentines: Actes du deuxième colloque international sur la littérature apocryphe chrétienne, Lausanne–Genève, 30 août–2 septembre 2006*. Frédéric Amsler et al., eds. Prahins: Éditions du Zèbre, 2008, 329–336.

Bowersock, Glen W. *Hellenism in Late Antiquity*, rev. ed. Ann Arbor: University of Michigan Press, 1996.
Bowie, Ewen L. "Hellenes and Hellenism in Writers of the Early Second Sophistic," in *ΕΛΛΗΝΙΣΜΟΣ*. Suzanne Saïd, ed. Leiden: Brill, 1991, 183–204.
Bowie, Ewen L. "The Ancient Readers of the Greek Novels," in *The Novel in the Ancient World*. Gareth Schmeling, ed. Leiden: Brill, 1996, 87–106.
Brant, Jo-Ann, Hedrick, Charles W., and Shea, Chris, eds. *Ancient Fiction: The Matrix of Early Christian and Jewish Narrative*. Atlanta: Society of Biblical Literature, 2005.
Bremmer, Jan N. "Achilles Tatius and Heliodorus in Christian East Syria," in *All Those Nations: Cultural Encounters within and with the Near East*. Herman L. J. Vanstiphout, ed. Groningen: Styx, 1999, 21–29.
Bremmer, Jan N. *The Pseudo-Clementines*. Leuven: Peeters, 2010a.
Bremmer, Jan N. "*Pseudo-Clementines*: Texts, Dates, Authors and Magic," in *The Pseudo-Clementines*. Jan N. Bremmer, ed. Leuven: Peeters, 2010b, 236–249.
Bremmer, Jan N. "Simon Magus: The Invention and Reception of a Magician in a Christian Context," *Religion in the Roman Empire* 5.2 (2019): 246–270.
Brod, Artemis. "The Upright Man: Favorinus, His Statue, and the Audience that Brought It Low," *Ancient Narrative* 15 (2019): 133–159.
Brown, Peter. *Power and Persuasion in Late Antiquity*. Madison: University of Wisconsin Press, 1992.
Calvet-Sebasti, Marie-Ange. "Femmes du roman pseudo-clémentin," in *Les Personnages du roman grec. Actes du colloque de Tours, 18–20 novembre 1999*. Bernard Pouderon, ed. Lyon: Maison de l'Orient et de la Méditerranée Jean Pouilloux, 2001, 285–297.
Calvet-Sébasti, Marie-Ange. "Une île romanesque: Arados," in *Lieux, décors et paysages de l'ancien roman des origines à Byzance*. Bernard Pouderon, ed. Lyon: Maison de l'Orient et de la Méditerranée Jean Pouilloux, 2005, 87–99.
Cambe, Michel. *Kerygma Petri: Textus et Commentarius*. Turnhout: Brepols, 2003.
Cameron, Averil. *Christianity and the Rhetoric of Empire: The Development of Christian Discourse*. Berkeley: University of California Press, 1991.
Carleton Paget, James. *Jews, Christians and Jewish Christians in Antiquity*. Tübingen: Mohr Siebeck, 2010.

Carlson, Donald H. *Jewish-Christian Interpretation of the Pentateuch in the Pseudo-Clementine Homilies*. Minneapolis: Fortress Press, 2013.

Cataudella, Quintino. "Vite di Santo e romanzo," Studi Ettore Paratore, 1981, 931–952.

Cerno, Marianna. *Un frammento inedito del romanzo su Clemente Romano*. Roma: Libreria Progetto, 2026, *forthcoming*.

Chapman, John. "On the Date of the Clementines," *Zeitschrift für die neutestamentliche Wissenschaft* 9 (1908a): 147–159.

Chapman, John. "Clementines," in *The Catholic Encyclopedia* [Vol. 4]. Charles G. Herbermann, ed. New York: Robert Appleton, 1908b, 39–44. Retrieved July 2, 2024 from New Advent: www.newadvent.org/cathen/04039b.htm.

Chariton. *Callirhoe,* edited and translated by George P. Goold. Cambridge: Harvard University Press, 1995.

Chawner, William. *Index of Noteworthy Words and Phrases Found in the Clementine Writings Commonly Called the Homilies of Clement*. London-New York: MacMillan, 1893.

Cirillo, Luigi. "Les sources du judéo-christianisme," *AEPHE/SSR* 83 (1974–1975): 235–242.

Cirillo, Luigi. "Jacques de Jérusalem d'après le roman du pseudo-Clément," in *La Figure du Prêtre dans les grandes traditions religieuses*. André Motte and Patrick Marchetti, eds. Leuven: Peeters, 2005, 177–188.

Cirillo, Luigi. "L'écrit pseudo-clémentin primitif ('Grundschrift'): Une apologie judéo-chrétienne et ses sources," In *Pierre Geoltrain, ou comment "faire l'histoire des religions?* Simon C. Mimouni and Isabelle Ullern-Weité, eds. Turnhout: Brepols, 2006, 223–237.

Cirillo, Luigi and Schneider, André. "Reconnaissances," in *Écrits Apocryphes Chrétiens II*. Pierre Geoltrain and Jean-Daniel Kaestli, eds. Paris: Gallimard, 2005.

Cooper, Kate. *The Virgin and the Bride: Idealized Womanhood in Late Antiquity*. Cambridge: Harvard University Press, 1996.

Côté, Dominique. *Le thème de l'opposition entre Pierre et Simon dans les Pseudo-Clémentines*. Paris: Institut d'Études Augustiniennes, 2001.

Côté, Dominique. "Les procédés rhét oriques dans les Pseudo-Clémentines: L'éloge de l'adultère du grammairien Apion," in *Nouvelles intrigues pseudo-clémentines. Actes du deuxième colloque international sur la littérature apocryphe chrétienne, Lausanne–Genève, 30 août–2 septembre 2006*. Frédéric Amsler et al., eds. Prahins: Éditions du Zèbre, 2008a, 189–210.

Côté, Dominique. "Les Pseudo-Clémentines et le choix du roman grec," in *Patristic Studies in the Twenty-First Century*. Brouria

Bitton-Ashkelony, Theodore de Bruyn, and Carol Harrison, eds. Turnhout: Brepols, 2008b, 473–496.

Côté, Dominique. *Pseudo-Clément et Vrai Prophète: Itinéraire de Rome à Jérusalem*. Turnhout: Brepols, 2022a.

Côté, Dominique. "La théogonie orphique des Pseudo-Clementines et la composition des Homélies et des Reconnaissances," *Apocrypha* 32 (2022b): 85–122.

Côté, Dominique. "Simon Magus in the Pseudo-Clementine Homilies: 'Magician' or Philosopher?" in *In Search of Truth in the Pseudo-Clementine Homilies: New Approaches to a Philosophical and Rhetorical Novel of Late Antiquity*. Benjamin M. J. De Vos and Danny Praet, eds. Tübingen: Mohr Siebeck, 2022c, 261–301.

Côté, Dominique. "Rufinus of Aquileia and the Reception of the Recognitions in Late Antiquity," in *Belief in/Believing Christian Narratives? Reading Strategies of Christian Fiction*. Benjamin M. J. De Vos, ed. 2025. Groningen: Barkhuis.

Cotelier, Jean-Baptiste. *SS. Patrum qui temporibus apostolicis floruerunt, Barnabae, Clementis, Hermae, Ignatii, Polycarpi opera edita et non edita, vera et supposita, graece et latine, cum notis*. Paris: Typis Petri Le Petit, 1672.

Crawford, Matthew R. "Κανών and Scripture according to the Letter of Peter to James," *Zeitschrift für Antikes Christentum* 20.2 (2016): 260–275.

Cullmann, Oscar. *Le problème littéraire et historique du roman pseudo-clémentin: Étude sur le rapport entre le gnosticisme et le Judéo-Christianisme*. Paris: Librairie Félix Alcan, 1930a.

Cullmann, Oscar. "Le problème littéraire et historique du roman pseudo-clémentin," *Revue d'histoire et de philosophie religieuses* 10 (4–5) (1930b): 471–476.

Czachesz, István, "The Clement Romance: Is It a Novel?" in *The Pseudo-Clementines*. Jan N. Bremmer, ed. Leuven: Peeters, 2010, 24–35.

de Lagarde, Paul A. *Clementis Romani Recognitiones Syriace*. Leipzig: F. A. Brockhaus/London: Williams & Norgate, 1861.

de Lagarde, Paul A. *Clementina*. Leipzig: F. A. Brockhaus, 1865.

De Temmerman, Koen. "Chaereas Revisited: Rhetorical Control in Chariton's 'Ideal' Novel Callirhoe," *Classical Quarterly* 59.1 (2009): 247–262.

De Temmerman, Koen. *Crafting Characters: Heroes and Heroines in the Ancient Greek Novel*. Oxford: Oxford University Press, 2014.

De Temmerman, Koen. "Ancient Biography and Formalities of Fiction," in *Writing Biography in Greece and Rome: Narrative Technique and*

Fictionalization. Koen De Temmerman and Kristoffel Demoen, eds. Cambridge: Cambridge University Press, 2016, 3–25.

De Temmerman, Koen. "Callirhoe and Euphemia" (unpublished presentation at the ICAN VI, Ghent), 2022.

De Vos, Benjamin M. J. "The Role of the Homilistic Disputes with Appion (*Klem.* 4–6)," *Vigiliae Christianae* 73.1 (2019): 54–88.

De Vos, Benjamin M. J. "The Disputes between Appion and Clement in the Pseudo-Clementine Homilies: A Narrative and Rhetorical Approach of the Structure of Hom. 6," *Ancient Narrative* 16 (2020): 81–109.

De Vos, Benjamin M. J. "The Pseudo-Clementine Homilies and the Art of 'Fake News': Deceptions and Dissimulations Aimed at the Gentile Audience," in *Polemics and Networking in Graeco-Roman Antiquity*. Pieter d'Hoine et al., eds. Turnhout: Brepols Publishers, 2021a, 423–459.

De Vos, Benjamin M. J. "The Literary Characterisation of Peter in the Pseudo-Clementine Homilies: Life-Guide, Rhetorician, and Philosopher," in *Peter in the Early Church: Apostle, Missionary, Church Leader*. Judith Lieu, ed. Leuven: Peeters, 2021b, 483–509.

De Vos, Benjamin M. J. "From the Dark Platonic Cave to the Vision of Beauty and the Act of ὁμοίωσις θεῷ: The Pseudo-Clementine Homilies as a Late Antique Philosophical Narrative," in *In Search of Truth in the Pseudo-Clementine Homilies: New Approaches to a Philosophical and Rhetorical Novel of Late Antiquity*. Benjamin M. J. De Vos and Danny Praet, eds. Tübingen: Mohr Siebeck, 2022, 221–260.

De Vos, Benjamin M. J. "Plato's Phaedrus and Symposium in the Pseudo-Clementine Homilies," *Zeitschrift für Antikes Christentum* 27.1 (2023): 102–146.

De Vos, Benjamin M. J. "Paideia, Plato's Sophist and the Pseudo-Clementines: Simon Magus' Characterisation in the Pseudo-Clementine Homilies," in *The Reception of Biblical Figures: Essays in Method*. David Hamidovic, Eleonora Serra, and Philippe Therrien, eds. Turnhout: Brepols, 2024a, 187–222.

De Vos, Benjamin M. J. "Living Philosophical Fiction: Plato's Myth of Er in the Clementina," *Hermathena* 207 (2024b): 53–84.

De Vos, Benjamin M. J. "The Pseudo-Clementine Lives of Eminent (and Less-Eminent) Philosophers, Sophists, and Physicians. Christian Paideia and Fictionalising Networks in the Late Ancient Novel," in *Doctrinal and Literary Strategies in Biographical Literature for Constructing Intellectual Networks from Antiquity to the Renaissance* [LECTIO]. Pieter D'Hoine et al., eds. Turnhout: Brepols, 2025a, *forthcoming*.

De Vos, Benjamin M. J. "The *Pseudo-Clementine Recognitions* as Early Christian Philosophy: Plato's Presence in the Construction of a Christian Philosophical Way of Life," *Harvard Theological Review* (2025b, *forthcoming*).

De Vos, Benjamin M. J. and Praet, Danny. "The Pseudo-Clementines: Title, Genre and Research Questions," in *In Search of Truth in the Pseudo-Clementine Homilies: New Approaches to a Philosophical and Rhetorical Novel of Late Antiquity*. Benjamin M. J. De Vos and Danny Praet, eds. Tübingen: Mohr Siebeck, 2022, 1–36.

Delling, Gerhard. "Philons Enkomion auf Augustus," *Klio* 54 (1972): 171–192.

DiRusso, Giovanni. "From Mournful Mattidia to Mitradora the Philosopher: Family Recognition, Authority, and Believability Across Arabic Pseudo-Clementine Literature," in *Belief in/Believing Christian Narratives? Reading Strategies of Christian Fiction*. Benjamin M. J. De Vos, ed. Groningen: Barkhuis, 2026, *forthcoming*.

Dressel, Albert R. M. *Clementis Romani Quae Feruntur Homiliae Viginti Nunc Primum Integrae*. Göttingen: Sumptibus Librariae Dieterichianae, 1853.

Dressel, Albert R. M. *Clementinorum Epitomae Duae*, altera edita correctior. Leipzig: J. C. Hinrichs, 1873.

Duncan, Patricia A. *Novel Hermeneutics in the Greek Pseudo-Clementine Romance*. Tübingen: Mohr Siebeck, 2017.

Duncan, Patricia A. "Eve, Mattidia, and the Gender Discourse of the Greek Pseudo-Clementine Novel," *Early Christianity* 11 (2020): 171–190.

Edwards, Mark J. "The Clementina: A Christian Response to the Pagan Novel," *Classical Quarterly* 42.2 (1992): 459–474.

Ehrenkrook, Jason von. "Christians, Pagans, and the Politics of Paideia in Late Antiquity," in *Second Temple Jewish 'Paideia' in Context*. Jason Zurawski and Gabriele Boccaccini, eds. Berlin: de Gruyter, 2017, 255–265.

Epiphanius. *Ancoratus und Panarion Haer. 1-33*. Karl Holl, ed. Leipzig: J. C. Hinrichs'sche Buchhandlung, 1915, 296–297 and 352.

Eshleman, Kendra. *The Social World of Intellectuals in the Roman Empire: Sophists, Philosophers, and Christians*. Cambridge: Cambridge University Press, 2012.

Eusebius Caesariensis. *Histoire Ecclésiastique*. Edité par Gustave Bardy [Sources Chrétiennes 41]. Paris: Les Éditions du Cerf, 1955, 31–32.

Filippini, Alister. "Atti apocrifi petrini: Note per una lettura storico-sociale degli Actus Vercellenses e del romanzo pseudo-clementino tra IV e V secolo," *Mediterraneo Antico* XI.1–2 (2008): 17–41.

Forger, Deborah. "Interpreting the Syrophoenician Woman to Construct Jewish-Christian Fault Lines: Chrysostom and the Ps-Cl Homilist in Chrono-Locational Perspective," *Journal of the Jesus Movement in Its Jewish Setting* 3 (2016): 132–166.

Frankenberg, Wilhelm. *Die syrischen Clementinen mit griechischen Paralleltext: Eine Vorarbeit zu dem literargeschichtlichen Problem der Sammlung.* Leipzig: J. C. Hinrichs, 1937.

Gebhardt, Joseph G. *The Syriac Clementine Recognitions and Homilies.* Nashville: Grave Distractions Publications, 2014.

Genette, Gérard. *Palimpsests: Literature in the Second Degree* (translated by C. Newman and C. Doubinsky). Lincoln-London: University of Nebraska Press, 1997.

Geoltrain, Pierre. "Le roman pseudo-clémentin depuis les recherches d'Oscar Cullmann," in *Le judéo-christianisme dans tous ses états: Actes du colloque de Jérusalem – 6–10 juillet 1998.* Simon C. Mimouni and Stanley F. Jones, eds. Paris: éditions du Cerf, 2001, 31–38.

Gregorius Nazianzus. "Oratio IV – Contra Julianum I," in *Patrologiae Cursus Completus seu Bibliotheca universalis, integra, uniformis, commoda, oeconomica omnium ss. patrum, doctorum, scriptorumque ecclesiasticorum sive Latinorum, sive Graecorum, qui ab aevo apostolico ad aetatem Innocentii III, pro Latinis et ad Photii tempora (ann. 863) pro Graecis floruerunt. Series Graeca. Patrologiae Graecae Tomus XXXV.* Jacques Paul Migne, ed. Paris: Petit-Montrouge, 1857, 633–649.

Gibson, Margaret D. *StSin 5: Apocrypha Sinaitica*, London: C. J. Clay and Sons, 1896.

Goldhill, Simon. *Foucault's Virginity: Ancient Erotic Fiction and the History of Sexuality.* Cambridge: Cambridge University Press, 1995.

Goldhill, Simon. *Being Greek under Rome: Cultural Identity, the Second Sophistic and the Development of Empire.* Cambridge: Cambridge University Press, 2001.

Haar, Stephen. *Simon Magus: The First Gnostic?* Berlin: De Gruyter, 2003.

Hägg, Tomas. *The Novel in Antiquity.* Berkeley: University of California Press, 1983.

Hansen, Dirk U. "Die Metamorphose des Heiligen Clemens und die Clementina," in *Groningen Colloquia on the Novel 8.* Heinz Hofmann and Maaike Zimmerman, eds. Groningen: Egbert Forsen, 1997, 119–129.

Harnack, Adolf von. *Dogmengeschichte* [Erster Band]. Freiburg: J. C. B. Mohr (Paul Siebeck), 1888.

Harris, Rendel. "Notes on the Clementine Romances," *Journal of Biblical Literature* 40.3–4 (1921): 125–145.

Hawk, Brandon. "The Pseudo-Clementines and the Canterbury School of Theodore and Hadrian in Early England" (Unpublished paper presented at NASSCAL First Friday Meetings 2023).

Haynes, Katharine. *Fashioning the Feminine in the Greek Novel*. London: Routledge, 2003.

Headlam, Arthur C. "The Clementine Literature," *Journal of Theological Studies* 3.9 (1901): 41–58.

Heintze, Werner. *Der Klemensroman und seine griechischen Quellen*. Leipzig: J. C. Hinrichs, 1914.

Hilgenfeld, Adolf. *Die Clementinischen Recognitionen und Homilien nach ihrem Ursprung und Inhalt dargestellt*. Jena: J. G. Schreiber, 1848.

Hogeterp, Albert L. A. "Judaism and Hellenism in the Pseudo-Clementine Homilies and the Canonical Acts of the Apostles," in *The Pseudo-Clementines*. Jan N. Bremmer, ed. Leuven: Peeters, 2010, 59–71.

Holzberg, Niklas. *The Ancient Novel: An Introduction* (translated by Christine Jackson-Holzberg). London-New York: Routledge, 1995.

Hort, Fenton J. A. *Judaistic Christianity: A Course of Lectures*. Cambridge-London: Macmillan, 1894.

Hunter, Richard. "Plato's Symposium and the Traditions of Ancient Fiction," in *Plato's Symposium: Issues in Interpretation and Reception*. James Lesher, Debra Nails, and Frisbee Sheffield, eds. Washington, DC: Center for Hellenic Studies, 2007, 295–312.

Hunter, Richard. "The Curious Incident…: Polypragmosune and the Ancient Novel," in *Readers and Writers in the Ancient Novel*. Stelios Panayotakis, Michael Paschalis, and Gareth Schmeling, eds. Groningen: Barkhuis, 2009, 51–63.

Hutt, Curtis. *The Sorrows of Mattidia: A New Translation and Commentary* (translated by Jenni Irving). London-New York: Routledge, 2019.

Hvalvik, Reidar and Sandnes, Karl O. "Pseudo-Klemens homilier," in *Tidligkristne apokryfer*. Reidar Aasgaard, ed. Oslo: De norske bokklubbene, 2011, 257–294.

Inglebert, Hervé. *Histoire de la civilisation romaine*. Paris: Presses Universitaires de France, 2005.

Irenaeus Lugdunensis. *Contre les Hérésies. Livre III*. Texte Latin, fragments grecs, introduction, traduction et notes de F. Sagnard, O.P. Paris: Les Éditions du Cerf, 1952, 105–108.

Irmscher, Johannes and Strecker, Georg. "Die Pseudoklementinen," in *Neutestamentliche Apokryphen in deutscher Übersetzung*, 5th ed. Wilhelm Schneemelcher and Edgar Hennecke, eds. Tübingen: Mohr Siebeck, 1989, 439–488.

Irmscher, Johannes and Strecker, Georg. "The Pseudo-Clementines," in *New Testament Apocrypha*. Wilhelm Schneemelcher, ed. and Robert McL. Wilson, trans. Louisville: Westminster John Knox Press, 2003, 483–541.

Iser, Wolfgang. *Der Akt des Lesens: Theorie ästhetischer Wirkung*. München: Fink, 1976.

Jaeger, Werner. *Paideia: The Ideals of Greek Culture* (translated from the Second German Edition by Gilbert Highet). New York: Oxford University Press, 1945.

Jaeger, Werner. "The Rhetoric of Isocrates and Its Cultural Ideal," in *Landmark Essays on Classical Greek Rhetoric*. Edward Schiappa, ed. Mahwah: Lawrence Erlbaum, 1994, 119–141.

Johnson, Scott F. "Christian Apocrypha," in *The Oxford Handbook of the Second Sophistic*. Daniel S. Richter and William A. Johnson, eds. Oxford: Oxford University Press, 2017, 669–686.

Jones, Stanley F. "The Pseudo-Clementines: A History of Research," *Second Century* 2 (1982): 1–33; 63–96.

Jones, Stanley F. "PsCl Concordances: Mistakes/Corrections," *Zeitschrift für Antikes Christentum* 1 (1997): 126–128.

Jones, Stanley F. "The Identities of the Pseudo-Clementine Authors," unpublished paper presented at the AELAC Annual Meeting, July 2, 2001, 9.

Jones, Stanley F. "Introduction to the Pseudo-Clementines," in *Pseudoclementina Elchasaiticaque inter Judaeochristiana: Collected Studies*. Stanley F. Jones, ed. Leuven: Peeters, 2012a, 3–49.

Jones, Stanley F. "Photius's Witness to the Pseudo-Clementines," in *Pseudoclementina Elchasaiticaque inter Judaeochristiana: Collected Studies*. Stanley F. Jones, ed. Leuven: Peeters, 2012b, 345–355.

Jones, Stanley F. "The Pseudo-Clementines: A History of Research," in *Pseudoclementina Elchasaiticaque inter Judaeochristiana: Collected Studies*. Stanley F. Jones, ed. Leuven: Peeters, 2012c, 50–113.

Jones, Stanley F. "Eros and Astrology in the Περίοδοι Πέτρου: The Sense of the Pseudo-Clementine Novel," in *Pseudoclementina Elchasaiticaque inter Judaeochristiana: Collected Studies*. Stanley F. Jones, ed. Leuven: Peeters, 2012d, 114–137.

Jones, Stanley F. "The Genesis of Pseudo-Clementine Christianity: Paper Presented for the Construction of Christian Identities Section at the 2009 Annual Meeting of the Society of Biblical Literature in New Orleans, LA," in *Pseudoclementina Elchasaiticaque inter Judaeochristiana: Collected Studies*. Stanley F. Jones, ed. Leuven: Peeters, 2012e, 204–206.

Jones, Stanley F. "Jewish Christianity of the Pseudo-Clementines," in *Pseudoclementina Elchasaiticaque inter Judaeochristiana: Collected Studies*. Stanley F. Jones, ed. Leuven: Peeters, 2012f, 138–151.

Jones, Stanley F. *The Syriac Pseudo-Clementines: An Early Version of the First Christian Novel*. Turnhout: Brepols, 2014.

Jones, Stanley F. "The Orphic Cosmo-Theogony in the Pseudo-Clementines," in *Les polémiques religieuses du Ier au IVe siècle de notre ère. Hommage à Bernard Pouderon*. Guillaume Bady and Diane Cuny, eds. Paris: Beauchesne, 2019a, 71–82.

Jones, Stanley F. "Novels," in *The Oxford Handbook of Early Christian Biblical Interpretation*. Paul M. Blowers and Peter W. Martens, eds. Oxford: Oxford University Press, 2019b, 295–302.

Kelley, Nicole. *Knowledge and Religious Authority in the Pseudo-Clementines: Situating the 'Recognitions' in Fourth Century Syria*. Tübingen: Mohr Siebeck, 2006.

Kelley, Nicole. "Astrology in the Pseudo-Clementine Recognitions," *Journal of Ecclesiastical History* 59.4 (2008): 607–629.

Kelley, Nicole. "On Recycling Texts and Traditions: The Pseudo-Clementine Recognitions and Religious Life in Fourth-Century Syria," in *The Levant: Crossroads of Late Antiquity: History, Religion and Archaeology*. Ellen B. Aitiken and John M. Fossey, eds. Leiden: Brill, 2014, 105–112.

Kennedy, George A. *Progymnasmata: Greek Textbooks of Prose Composition and Rhetoric*, Leiden: Brill, 2003.

Kerényi, Karl. *Die griechisch-orientalische Romanliteratur in religionsgeschichtlicher Beleuchtung: Ein Versuch mit Nachbetrachtungen*. Darmstadt: Wissenschaftliche Buchgesellschaft, 1962 (1927).

Keydell, Rudolf. "Zur Datierung der Aithiopika Heliodors," in *Polychronion: Festschrift Franz Dölger zum 75. Geburtstag*. Peter Wirth, ed. Heidelberg: C. Winter, 1966, 345–350.

Kilgour, Maggie. *From Communion to Cannibalism: An Anatomy of Metaphors of Incorporation*. Princeton: Princeton University Press, 1990.

König, Jason. "Favorinus' 'Corinthian Oration' in Its Corinthian Context," *Proceedings of the Cambridge Philological Society* 47 (2001): 141–171.

König, Jason. "Novelistic and Anti-Novelistic Narrative in The Acts of Thomas and The Acts of Andrew and Matthias," in *Fiction on the Fringe: Novelistic Writing in the Post-Classical Age*. Karla Grammatiki, ed. Leiden-Boston: Brill, 2009, 121–149.

Konstan, David. *Sexual Symmetry: Love in the Ancient Novel and Related Genres*. Princeton: Princeton University Press, 1994.

Kruchió, Benedek. "Heliodorus. Greek Novelist c. 4th century CE," in *Oxford Classical Dictionary*, 2016. Retrieved March 3, 2024.

Langen, Joseph. *Die Klemensromane: Ihre Entstehung und ihre Tendenzen aufs neue untersucht*. Gotha: Friedrich Andreas Perthes, 1890.

Le Boulluec, Alain et al., eds. "Homélies de Pseudo-Clément," in *Écrits Apocryphes Chrétiens II*. Pierre Geoltrain et al., eds. Paris: Gallimard, 2005, 1215–1589.

Le Boulluec, Alain. "La Monarchia dans les Homélies Clémentines et l'origine du Mauvais," *Chôra* 13 (2015): 437–450.

Lipsius, Richard A. *Die Quellen der römischen Petrus-Sage*. Kiel: Schwers'sche Buchhandlung, 1872.

Liverani, Paolo. "Pietro Turista. La visita ad Arado secondo le Pseudo-Clementine," in *Il contributo delle scienze storiche allo studio del nuovo testamento: Atti del Convegno Roma, 2–6 ottobre 2002*. Enrico D. Covolo and Roberto Fusco, eds. Vatican City: Libreria Editrice Vaticana, 2005, 136–145.

Lorenz, Rudolph. *Arius Judaizans? Untersuchungen zur dogmengeschichtlichen Einordnung des Arius*. Göttingen: Vandenhoeck & Ruprecht, 1979.

Maistre, Étienne. *Saint Clément de Rome: Son histoire renfermant les Actes de Saint Pierre, ses écrits avec les preuves qui les réhabilitent, son glorieux martyre* [2 Vol.]. Paris: F. Wattelier, 1883–1884.

Manns, Frédéric. "Les Pseudo-Clémentines (*Homélies* et *Reconnaissances*). État de la question," *Liber Annuus* 53 (2003): 157–184.

Marrou, Henri-Irénée. *Histoire de l'éducation dans l'Antiquité*. Paris: Seuil, 1948.

Marti, Heinrich. "Ordo – ein Grundprinzip erfolgreicher Katechese," in *Nouvelles intrigues pseudo-clémentines. Actes du deuxième colloque international sur la littérature apocryphe chrétienne, Lausanne–Genève, 30 août–2 septembre 2006*. Frédéric Amsler et al., eds. Prahins: Éditions du Zèbre, 2008, 235–240.

McGill, Scott and Watts, Edward J., eds. *A Companion to Late Antique Literature*. New York: Wiley, 2018.

Merkelbach, Reinhold. *Roman und Mysterium in der Antike*. München-Berlin: Beck, 1962.

Messis, Charis. "Fiction and/or Novelisation in Byzantine Hagiography," in *The Ashgate Research Companion to Byzantine Hagiography Volume II: Genres and Contexts*. Stephanos Efthymiadeis, ed. Farnham: Ashgate, 2014, 313–342.

Messis, Charis and Papaioannou, Stratis. "Histoires 'gothiques' à Byzance: Le saint, le soldat et le Miracle d'Euphémie et du Goth (BHG 739)," *Dumbarton Oaks Papers* 67 (2013): 15–47.

Meyboom, Hajo U. *De Clemens-Roman: Synoptische Vertaling van den Tekst*. Groningen: J. B. Wolters, 1902.
Molland, Einar. "La circoncision, le baptême et l'autorité du décret apostolique (Actes XV, 28 sq.) dans les milieux judéo-chrétiens des Pseudo-Clémentines," *Studia Theologica* 9 (1955): 1–39.
Momigliano, Arnaldo. *Alien Wisdom: The Limits of Hellenization*. Cambridge: Cambridge University Press, 1998 [1971].
Montiglio, Silvia. *Love and Providence: Recognition in the Ancient Novel*. Oxford: Oxford University Press, 2012.
Montiglio, Silvia. "Chariclea's Beauty: A Light without Colors or Shapes" (unpublished presentation at the ICAN VI, Ghent, 2022).
Morales, Helen. *Vision and Narrative in Achilles Tatius' Leucippe and Clitophon*. Cambridge: Cambridge University Press, 2004.
Morgan, John R. "Make Believe and Make-Believe: The Fictionality of the Greek Novels," in *Lies and Fiction in the Ancient World*. Christopher Gill and Timothy P. Wiseman, eds. Austin: University of Texas Press, 1993, 175–229.
Morgan, John R. "Heliodorus," in *The Novel in the Ancient World*. Gareth L. Schmeling, ed. Boston-Leiden: Brill, 1996, 417–456.
Nasrallah, Laura. "Mapping the World: Justin, Tatian, Lucian, and the Second Sophistic," *Harvard Theological Review* 98 (2005): 283–314.
Neander, August. *Genetische Entwicklung der vornehmsten gnostischen Systeme*. Berlin: Ferdinand Dümmler, 1818.
Nicklas, Tobias. "Apocryphal Jesus Stories in the Pseudo-Clementine Homilies: The Syrophoenician Woman (Hom. 219) and the Dispute with the Sadducees (Hom. 3.50.1 and 3.54.2)," in *In Search of Truth in the Pseudo-Clementine Homilies: New Approaches to a Philosophical and Rhetorical Novel of Late Antiquity*. Benjamin M. J. De Vos and Danny Praet, eds. Tübingen: Mohr Siebeck, 2022, 131–144.
Nilsson, Ingela. "Desire and God Have Always Been Around, in Life and Romance Alike," in *Plotting with Eros: Essays on the Poetics of Love and the Erotics of Reading*. Ingela Nilsson, ed. Copenhagen: Museum Tusculanum Press, 2009, 235–260.
Nöldeke, Theodor. "Bar Choni über Homer, Hesiod und Orpheus," *Zeitschrift der Deutschen Morgenländischen Gesellschaft* 53 (1899): 501–507.
Norelli, Enrico. "Situation des apocryphes pétriniens," *Apocrypha* 2 (1991), 31–83.
North, Helen F. *Sophrosyne: Self-knowledge and Self-restraint in Greek Literature*. Ithaca: Cornell University Press, 1966.

Paschke, Franz. *Die beiden griechischen Klementinen-Epitomen und ihre Anhänge: Überlieferungsgeschichtliche Vorarbeiten zu einer Neuausgabe der Texte*. Berlin: Akademie-Verlag, 1966.

Pernot, Laurent. "Greek and Latin Rhetorical Culture," in *The Oxford Handbook to the Second Sophistic*. Daniel S. Richter and William A. Johnson, eds. Oxford: Oxford University Press, 2017, 205–216.

Pernot, Laurent. "The Concept of a Third Sophistic: Definitional and Methodological Issues," *Rhetorica* 39.2 (2021): 177–187.

Perry, Ben E. *The Ancient Romances: A Literary–Historical Account of Their Origins*. Berkeley-Los Angeles: University Press, 1967.

Pervo, Richard. "The Ancient Novel Becomes Christian," in *The Novel in the Ancient World*. Gareth Schmeling, ed. Leiden: Brill, 1996, 685–711.

Petersmann, Hubert. "Zur Entstehung der hellenistischen Koine," *Philologus* 139 (1995): 3–14.

Piñero, Antonio and del Cerro, Gonzalo, eds. *Hechos apócrifos de los Apóstoles IVa. La novela de Clemente. Disputa de Pedro con Simón Mago*. Madrid: Biblioteca de Autores Cristianos, 2023.

Pinheiro, Marília P. F., Perkins, Judith, and Pervo, Richard, eds. *The Ancient Novel and Early Christian and Jewish Narrative: Fictional Intersections*. Groningen: Barkhuis, 2012.

Plato. *Lysis, Symposium, Phaedrus*. Edited and translated by Christopher Emlyn-Jones. Cambridge: Harvard University Press, 2022, 510–526.

Pouderon, Bernard. "Faust, le Faustbuch et le Faustus Pseudo-Clémentin, ou la genèse d'un mythe," *Revue des Études Grecques* 121.1 (2008): 127–148.

Pouderon, Bernard. "Origène, le pseudo-Clément et la structure des Periodoi Petrou," in *La genèse du roman pseudo-clémentin: Études littéraires et historiques*. Bernard Pouderon, ed. Paris-Leuven-Walpole: Peeters, 2012a, 87–103.

Pouderon, Bernard. "Aux origines du roman clémentin: Prototype païen, refonte judéo-hellénistique, remaniement chrétien," in *La genèse du roman pseudo-clémentin: Études littéraires et historiques*. Bernard Pouderon, ed. Paris-Leuven-Walpole: Peeters, 2012b, 21–48.

Pouderon, Bernard. "La genèse du Roman Pseudo-Clémentin et sa signification théologique," in *La genèse du roman pseudo-clémentin: Études littéraires et historiques*. Bernard Pouderon, ed. Paris-Leuven-Walpole: Peeters, 2012c, 313–337.

Pouderon, Bernard. *Métamorphoses de Simon le magicien: Des Actes des apôtres au Faustbuch*. Paris: Beauchesne, 2019.

Praet, Danny. "Truth-telling, Lying and False Wisdom in the Pseudo-Clementine Homilies: Simon Magus and Helen of Troy," in *In Search *of Truth in the Pseudo-Clementine Homilies: New Approaches to a Philosophical and Rhetorical Novel of Late Antiquity*. Benjamin M. J. De Vos and Danny Praet, eds. Tübingen: Mohr Siebeck, 2022, 189–220.

Rappe, Sara. "The New Math: How to Add and to Subtract Pagan Elements in Christian Education," in *Education in Greek and Roman Antiquity*. Yun Lee Too, ed. Leiden-Boston-Köln: Brill, 2001, 405–432.

Reardon, Bryan P., ed. *Collected Ancient Greek Novels*. Berkeley: University of California Press, 1989.

Reed, Annette Y. "'Jewish Christianity' after the 'Parting of the Ways': Approaches to Historiography and Self-Definition in the Pseudo-Clementines," in *The Ways that Never Parted: Jews and Christians in Late Antiquity and the Early Middle Ages*. Adam H. Becker and Annette Y. Reed, eds. Tübingen: Mohr Siebeck, 2003, 189–231.

Reed, Annette Y. "Reflections on F. Stanley Jones, Pseudoclementina Elchasaiticaque inter Judaeochristiana: Collected Studies," *Annali di Storia dell' Esegesi* 30.1 (2013): 93–101.

Reed, Annette Y. *Jewish-Christianity and the History of Judaism*. Tübingen: Mohr Siebeck, 2018.

Rehm, Bernhard and Strecker, Georg. *Die griechischen christlichen Schriftsteller der ersten Jahrhunderte. Die Pseudoklementinen I. Homilien*. Berlin: Akademie Verlag, 1992³.

Rehm, Bernhard and Strecker, Georg. *Die griechischen christlichen Schriftsteller der ersten Jahrhunderte. Die Pseudoklementinen II. Rekognitionen in Rufins Übersetzung*. Berlin: Akademie Verlag, 1994².

Rehm, Bernhard. "Zur Entstehung der pseudoclementinischen Schriften," *Zeitschrift für die neutestamentliche Wissenschaft* 37 (1938a): 77–184.

Rehm, Bernhard. "Bardesanes in den Pseudoclementinen," *Philologus* 93 (1938b): 218–247.

Rehm, Bernhard. "Clemens Romanus II (PsClementinen)," in *Reallexikon für Antike und Christentum* [3 Vol.]. Theodor Klauser, ed. Stuttgart: Hiersemann Verlags-G.M.B.H., 1957, 197–206.

Rimell, Victoria. *Petronius and the Anatomy of Fiction*. Cambridge: Cambridge University Press, 2002.

Risch, Frank X. *Die Pseudoklementinen IV: Die Klemens-Biographie: Epitome prior, Martyrium Clementis, Miraculum Clementis*. Berlin: de Gruyter, 2008.

Rius-Camps, Josep. "Las Pseudoclementinas: Bases filológicas para una nueva interpretación," *Revista Catalana de Teologia* 1 (1976): 79–158.

Roberts, Alexander and Donaldson, James. *Ante-Nicene Christian Library: Translations of the Writings of the Fathers Down to A.D. 325.*

Vol. XVII. The Clementine Homilies, the Apostolical Constitutions. Edinburgh: T&T Clark, 1870, 1–340.

Rochet, Bruno. "Remarques sur l'élaboration de la conscience linguistique des Grecs," *Glotta* 79.1–4 (2003): 175–204.

Rohde, Erwin. *Der griechische Roman und seine Vorläufer.* Hildesheim-New York: Georg Olms Verlag, 1974 (1876).

Salles, Antoine. "Simon le magicien ou Marcion?" *Vigiliae Christianae* 12 (1958): 197–224.

Salač, Antonin. "Die Pseudoklementinen und ein griechischer Liebesroman," *Listy filologické* 82.2 (1959): 45–49.

Schliemann, Adolph. *Die Clementinen nebst den verwandten Schriften und der Ebionitismus: Ein Beitrag zur Kirchen–und Dogmengeschichte der ersten Jahrhunderte.* Hamburg: Friedrich Perthes, 1844.

Schmeling, Gareth. "Callirhoe: God-like Beauty and the Making of a Celebrity," in *Metaphor and the Ancient Novel.* Stephen Harrison, Michael Paschalis, and Stavros Frangoulidis, eds. Groningen: Barkhuis, 2005, 36–49.

Schmidt, Carl. *Studien zu den Pseudo-Clementinen nebst einem Anhange: Die älteste römische Bischofsliste und die Pseudo-Clementinen.* Leipzig: J. C. Hinrichs, 1929.

Schneemelcher, Wilhelm. "Das Kerygma Petri," in *Neutestamentliche Apokryphen in deutscher Übersetzung. Vol 2: Apostolisches, Apokalypsen und Verwandtes.* 5th ed. Wilhelm Schneemelcher, ed. Tübingen: Mohr Siebeck, 1989, 34–41.

Schoeps, Hans-Joachim. "Astrologisches im pseudoklementinischen Roman," *Vigiliae Christianae* 5.2 (1951a): 88–100.

Schoeps, Hans-Joachim. "Die Pseudoklementinen und das Urchristentum," *Zeitschrift für Religions- und Geistesgeschichte* 10 (1951b): 3–15.

Scholem, Gershom. *On the Kabbalah and Its Symbolism* (translated by Ralph Manheim). New York: Schocken Books, 1965.

Schwartz, Eduard. "Unzeitgemässe Beobachtungen zu den Clementinen," *Zeitschrift für die neutestamentliche Wissenschaft* 31 (1932): 151–199.

Schwegler, Albert. *Clementis Romani quae feruntur Homiliae.* Stuttgart: A. Becker, 1847.

Shuve, Karl E. The Pseudo-Clementine Homilies and the Antiochene Polemic against Allegory. McMaster University: Unpublished MA dissertation, 2007.

Siouville, André. *Les Homélies Clémentines.* Paris: Les Éditions Rieder, 1933.

Snyder, Glenn E. *Acts of Paul: The Formation of a Pauline Corpus*. Tübingen: Mohr Siebeck, 2013.

Stanton, Graham. "Jewish Christian Elements in the Pseudo-Clementine Writings," in *Jewish Believers in Jesus: The Early Centuries*. O. Skarsaune and Reidar Hvalvik, eds. Peabody: Hendrickson, 2007, 305–324.

Strecker, Georg. *Das Judenchristentum in den Pseudoklementinen*. Berlin: Akademie-Verlag, 1981, 137–138.

Strecker, Georg. *Die Pseudoklementinen III: Konkordanz zu den Pseudoklementinen* [2 Vol.]. Berlin: Akademie, 1986–1988.

Strohm, Hans. "' Hellenisch' als Wertbegriff. Beobachtungen zum hellenischen Kulturbewusstsein," *WHB* 24 (1983): 1–13.

Svennung, Josef. "Handschriften zu den pseudoklementinischen Recognitiones," *Philologus* 88 (1933): 473–476.

Teeple, Howard M. *The Prophet in the Clementines*. Evanston: Religion and Ethics Institute, 1933.

Therrien, Philippe. Gnose, narration et interprétation des Écritures dans les Pseudo-Clémentines. Une comparaison avec les écrits gnostiques [Thèse en cotutelle]. Université de Lausanne/Université Laval, 2024.

Timotin, Andrei. "Σοφία barbare et παιδεία grecque dans le Discours aux Hellènes de Tatien," in *Alexandrie la Divine. Sagesses barbares. Échanges et reappropriation dans l'espace culturel gréco-romain*. Sydney Hervé, ed. Genève: La Baconnière, 2016, 553–574.

Trenkner, Sophie. *The Greek Novella in the Classical Period*. Cambridge: Cambridge University Press, 1958.

Turrianus, Franciscus. *Adversus Magdeburgenses Centuriatores pro Canonibus Apostolorum, & Epistolis Decretalibus Pontificum Apostolocorum. Libri Quinque*. Florende: Ex Officina Bartholomaei Sermartelli, 1572.

Uhlhorn, Gerhard. *Die Homilien und Recognitionen des Clemens Romanus nach ihrem Ursprung und Inhalt dargestellt*. Göttingen: Verlag der Dieterichschen Buchhandlung, 1854.

Ullmann, Walter. "The Significance of the Epistola Clementis in the Pseudo-Clementines," *Journal of Theological Studies* 11 (1960): 295–317.

Ullmann, Walter. "Some Remarks on the Significance of the Epistola Clementis in the Pseudo-Clementines," *Studia Patristica* 4 (1961): 330–337.

Urbano, Arthur. *The Philosophical Life, Biography and the Crafting of Intellectual Identity in Late Antiquity*. Washington, DC: The Catholic University of America Press, 2013.

Vähäkangas, Païvi. "Christian Identity and Intra-Christian Polemics in the Pseudo-Clementines," in *Others and the Construction of Early*

Christian Identities. Raimo Hakola et al., eds. Helsinki: The Finnish Exegetical Society, 2013, 217–235.

Van Pelt, Julie. *Saints in Disguise: Performance, Illusion and Truth in Early Byzantine Hagiography*. Leuven: Peeters, 2024.

Van Pelt, Julie, De Temmerman, Koen, and Staat, Klazina, eds. *Narrative, Imagination and Concepts of Fiction in Late Antique Hagiography*. Leiden: Brill, 2023.

Vidalis, Markos. "Éléments liturgiques dans le roman pseudo-clémentin," in *Nouvelles intrigues pseudo-clémentines. Actes du deuxième colloque international sur la littérature apocryphe chrétienne, Lausanne–Genève, 30 août–2 septembre 2006*. Frédéric Amsler et al., eds. Prahins: Éditions du Zèbre, 2008, 259–268.

Vielberg, Meinolf. "Bildung und Rhetorik in den Pseudoklementinen," in *Antike Rhetorik und ihre Rezeption. Symposium zu Ehren von Professor Dr. Carl Joachim Classen, D. Litt. Oxon. am 21. und 22. November 1998 in Göttingen*. Siegmar Döpp, ed. Stuttgart: Steiner, 1999, 41–63.

Vielberg, Meinolf. *Klemens in den pseudoklementinischen Rekognitionen: Studien zur literarischen Form des spätantiken Romans*. Berlin: Akademie-Verlag, 2000.

Vielberg, Meinolf. "Rhetoric in the Ancient and Christian Novel: A Comparison between the Petronian Satyricon and the Pseudo-Clementine Homilies," in *In Search of Truth in the Pseudo-Clementine Homilies: New Approaches to a Philosophical and Rhetorical Novel of Late Antiquity*. Benjamin M. J. De Vos and Danny Praet, eds. Tübingen: Mohr Siebeck, 2022, 145–162.

Waitz, Hans. *Die Pseudoklementinen, Homilien und Rekognitionen: Eine Quellenkritische Untersuchung*. Leipzig. J. C. Hinrichs, 1904.

Wallace-Hadrill, Andrew. *Rome's Cultural Revolution*. Cambridge: Cambridge University Press, 2008.

Webb, Ruth. "Rhetoric and the Novel: Sex, Lies and Sophistic," in *A Companion to Greek Rhetoric*. Ian Worthington, ed. Malden: Wiley-Blackwell, 2007, 526–541.

Wehnert, Jürgen. "Literarkritik und Sprachanalyse: Kritische Anmerkungen zum gegenwärtigen Stand der Pseudoklementinen-Forschung," *Zeitschrift für die neutestamentliche Wissenschaft* 74 (1983): 268–301.

Wehnert, Jürgen. "Abriss der Entstehungsgeschichte des pseudoklementinischen Romans," *Apocrypha* 3 (1992): 211–235.

Wehnert, Jürgen. *Pseudoklementinische Homilien: Einführung und Übersetzung*. Göttingen: Vandenhoeck & Ruprecht, 2010.

Wehnert, Jürgen. *Der Klemensroman*. Göttingen: Vandenhoeck & Ruprecht, 2015.
Weinreich, Otto. *Der griechische Liebesroman*. Zürich: Artemis, 1962.
Whitmarsh, Tim. "'Greece is the World:' Exile and Identity in the Second Sophistic," in *Being Greek under Rome: Cultural Identity, the Second Sophistic and the Development of Empire*. Simon Goldhill, ed. Cambridge: Cambridge University Press, 2001a, 269–305.
Whitmarsh, Tim. *Greek Literature and the Roman Empire: The Politics of Imitation*. Oxford-New York: Oxford University Press, 2001b.
Whitmarsh, Tim. "The Greek Novel: Titles and Genre," *The American Journal of Philology* 126.4 (2005): 587–611.
Whitmarsh, Tim., ed. *The Cambridge Companion to the Greek and Roman Novel*. Cambridge: Cambridge University Press, 2008.
Whitmarsh, Tim. *Narrative and Identity in the Ancient Greek Novel: Returning Romance. Greek Culture in the Roman World*. Cambridge-New York: Cambridge University Press, 2011.
Wilken, Robert L. *John Chrysostom and the Jews: Rhetoric and Reality in the Late 4th Century*. Eugene: Wipf & Stock Publishers, 2004.
Zambon, Marco. "Apprendere qualcosa di sicuro (ps. Clem. *Klem.* I 2, 1). Verità filosofica e verità nella I omelia pseudoclementina," *Studia graeco-arabica* 8 (2018): 13–48.
Zeitlin, Froma. "Living Portraits and Sculpted Bodies in Chariton's Theater of Romance," in *The Ancient Novel and Beyond*. Maaike Zimmerman, ed. Leiden: Brill, 2003, 71–83.
Zosimus. "Epistula Secunda," in *Patrologiae Cursus Completus, sive Bibliotheca universalis, integra, uniformis, commoda, oeconomica, omnium ss. Patrum, doctorum scriptorumque ecclesiasticorum qui ab aevo apostolico ad usque Innocentii III tempora floruerunt. Series prima* [a Tertulliano ad Gregorium Magnum], *Patrologiae Tomus XX*. Jacques Paul Migne, ed. Paris: Petit-Montrouge, 1845, 650.

To Lore, and to my parents, with love and appreciation

Cambridge Elements

Early Christian Literature

Garrick V. Allen
University of Glasgow

Garrick V. Allen (PhD St Andrews, 2015) is Professor of Divinity and Biblical Criticism at the University of Glasgow. He is the author of multiple articles and books on the New Testament, early Jewish and Christian literature, and ancient and medieval manuscript traditions, including *Manuscripts of the Book of Revelation: New Philology, Paratexts, Reception* (Oxford University Press, 2020) and *Words are Not Enough: Paratexts, Manuscripts, and the Real New Tesatament* (Eerdmans, 2024). He is the winner of the Manfred Lautenschlaeger Award for Theological Promise and the Paul J. Achetemeier Award for New Testament Scholarship.

About the Series

This series sets new research agendas for understanding early Christian literature, exploring the diversity of Christian literary practices through the contexts of ancient literary production, the forms of literature composed by early Christians, themes related to particular authors, and the languages in which these works were written.

Cambridge Elements

Early Christian Literature

Elements in the Series

The Author in Early Christian Literature
Chance E. Bonar

Maximos the Confessor: Androprimacy and Sexual Difference
Luis Josué Salés

Egeria: Theological and Ecclesial Knowledge Between Eastern and Western Traditions
Anni Maria Laato

The Pseudo-Clementine *Tradition*
Benjamin M. J. De Vos

A full series listing is available at: www.cambridge.org/EECL

For EU product safety concerns, contact us at Calle de José Abascal, 56–1°, 28003 Madrid, Spain or eugpsr@cambridge.org.

www.ingramcontent.com/pod-product-compliance
Lightning Source LLC
LaVergne TN
LVHW011848060526
838200LV00054B/4237